DEVELOPING COMMUNICATION SKILLS

GENERAL CONSIDERATIONS
AND
SPECIFIC TECHNIQUES

Elizabeth Garner Joiner

University of South Carolina

Patricia Barney Westphal

University of Northern Iowa

Editors

NEWBURY HOUSE / ROWLEY / MASSACHUSETTS

Library of Congress Cataloging in Publication Data

Main entry under title:

Developing communication skills.

    Includes bibliographical references.
     1. Languages, Modern--Study and teaching.
2. Communication--Study and teaching. I. Joiner,
Elizabeth G. II. Westphal, Patricia Barney.
PB36.D44   418   78-16787
ISBN 0-88377-118-7

Cover design by Barbara Frake.

NEWBURY HOUSE PUBLISHERS, INC.

Language Science
Language Teaching
Language Learning

ROWLEY, MASSACHUSETTS 01969

First printing: October 1978
Printed in the U.S.A.   5   4   3   2   1

CONTENTS

ACKNOWLEDGMENTS

The editors are grateful to the authors who agreed to allow us to reprint or publish for the first time the articles included in this collection. We also thank the publishers who granted us permission to reprint material which appeared for the first time in their journals. Dianne Faver, Laura Shull, and Ursula Barrow helped with the typing of portions of the manuscript. Our special thanks to them and to Gloria Rogers and Deborah Davis, who acted as proofreaders.

ABOUT THIS BOOK

This book is, first and foremost, a practical book designed for the classroom teacher of a second or foreign language at any level. It may be regarded as a handbook of sorts for the teacher who would like for his students to be able to exchange ideas in the foreign language but who may have thus far been disappointed in his attempts to achieve this goal. Teacher trainers, too, who have come away from conferences and workshops with unanswered questions about the term *communicative competence* will find here a collection of articles on the topic to read and reflect upon at their leisure.

The articles selected for this collection have been grouped into two distinct but interdependent sections: Part I (General Considerations) and Part II (Specific Techniques). While articles in the first section are more theoretical than those in the second, each principle or concept is amply illustrated so that its applicability to the classroom can readily be seen. The authors treat a variety of topics including linguistic versus communicative competence, error correction, classroom atmosphere, textbook consideration and testing. Articles selected for Part II describe in detail classroom-tested activities which have proved effective in developing the ability to communicate in a foreign language. Included are small-group techniques, simulation and role-playing strategies, activities built around games and puzzles, and techniques based upon values clarification. The majority of the activities described would be most appropriately used at the beginning and intermediate levels of instruction although some would be appropriate for advanced students. While it is not necessary to read Part I before Part II, the reader who has a good understanding of the theory of *communicative competence* will be able to examine the techniques derived from this theory more critically than one who does not.

Hoping to provoke further reflection and investigation, we have included at the end of each section topics for discussion and suggestions for classroom application of the ideas presented in the readings. These questions were designed not only to point out fruitful areas of discussion within a given section but also to make the reader aware of the interrelatedness of the two sections.

We hope that our book will not only equip its readers with practical techniques to improve their efforts at promoting communication but that it will also stimulate them to experiment informally in their own classrooms with ideas they have encountered here. No one yet has all the answers to the question: "How do we develop the ability to communicate in a second language?" We invite you, our reader, to join us and the authors of the articles of this collection in the search for better and more complete answers.

Elizabeth G. Joiner
University of South Carolina

Patricia B. Westphal
University of Northern Iowa

GENERAL
CONSIDERATIONS

INTRODUCTION

The articles included in this first section treat a variety of topics of concern to the teacher who seriously wishes to help his students develop greater skill in communicating in a second language. In selecting these somewhat general articles, we attempted to choose only those which contained ample illustrations of how theory can be translated into practice. Our authors know the classroom first-hand and never stray far from it even in the treatment of complex and sometimes abstract theoretical concepts.

The first four articles define and establish the need for communicative language practice and treat such topics as classroom atmosphere, motivation and error correction. Westphal reports research which vividly shows that we must change our approach if we are to prepare students linguistically to function on their own in the real world. A direction for change is provided by Savignon, who stresses the need for giving students specific linguistic and nonlinguistic tools in addition to opportunities to engage in communicative behavior. Paulston in her analysis of oral language practice classifies structural pattern drills as mechanical, meaningful and communicative and points out the importance of progressing to the level of communicative drill. This analysis is further elaborated by Paulston and Selekman who integrate Paulston's classification with Rivers' skill-getting versus skill-using model.*

The articles by Zelson, Palmer, and Slager offer models for developing activities which should lead to success in communicating. While the interplay of structure and context in drills and exercises is treated

---

*"Talking Off the Tops of Their Heads" in W.M. Rivers, *Speaking in Many Tongues,* expanded 2d ed. (Rowley, Mass.: Newbury House, 1976), p. 23.

differently by each author, all agree that context cannot be ignored in communicative language practice.

Valette is the only author who specifically treats the problems of evaluating students' success in achieving communication skills. Because her article deals with skill development as well, it seems well-placed at the end of Part I as a kind of summary of the section.

While they are wide-ranging and varied, the articles of this section should equip the reader with a good working definition of the term *communication* as it relates to oral language practice and with a theoretical framework which he can draw upon as he reads the selections included in Part II.

Because we have chosen to focus on classroom language practice we have omitted from this collection a number of very fine articles on testing, research, and related topics which may be of interest to our readers. We have, for this reason, provided at the end of this section a list of suggested additional reading.

MOI TARZAN, VOUS JANE?
A STUDY OF COMMUNICATIVE COMPETENCE

Patricia B. Westphal
University of Northern Iowa

From *Foreign Language Annals,* vol. 8, no. 1 (March 1975), pp. 38-42.

Although it is commonly accepted that the ability to communicate is a primary goal of foreign language instruction, there appears to be no detailed study of how students actually perform in a communicative act. We assume that skills developed in the performance of pattern drills, dialogue acquisition, and various other kinds of oral classroom activities transfer to "real" settings, but we have little empirical support for this assumption. If suddenly transported to a foreign country, would a student's foreign language be some kind of "Me Tarzan, you Jane" variety? Would his language resemble a pidgin, an early child language, or might it have unique characteristics?

The results of studies of the child's acquisition of his native language have led theorists to hypothesize similar processes in second language acquisition: the second language learner produces a language more and more closely resembling that of a native speaker as he adopts successive interim grammars, which are defined by his errors. Valdman argues that "when their natural language learning strategies are allowed to operate without external interference, such as that of the teacher, these learners restructure foreign language data into simpler systems which they can handle better in the communication of meaningful linguistic messages."[1] What does a student really learn about communication in a foreign language and how would he apply what he has learned if given the opportunity?

The present study was conceived to provide information about the grammatical structures students use in a conversational setting, and about the relationship between the appearance of structures and seven independent variables usually associated with success in foreign language.

Two hundred twenty-three volunteers near the end of their second year of French in fourteen secondary schools in the Columbus, Ohio, area conducted individual oral interviews with the researcher, who posed as Jacqueline LaPorte, a French girl who spoke no English. During the interview each subject attempted, by interrogating Jacqueline in French, to gather these fourteen bits of information:

(1) If she has any brothers or sisters;
(2) What their names are;
(3) Where her parents are;
(4) If her mother is shorter or taller than the interviewer is;
(5) Where she was born (city);
(6) What she did on Sundays when she was a little girl;
(7) Why she doesn't speak English;
(8) If she drinks coffee or wine with meals;
(9) Where she's going to spend next summer;
(10) What she wants to see most in America;
(11) When she has to leave for France;
(12) If she would stay in America if she could;
(13) If the French government sent her;
(14) Where she would like to live.

The tape-recorded interviews, which provided the corpus for the study, were analyzed to determine which correct forms and which errors occurred with a frequency of at least 22. (This figure was arbitrarily set in an effort to eliminate nonce errors from the corpus.) Chi-square tests for statistical independence were then applied to each of these forms, using seven independent variables: school attended, previous language experience, willingness to persevere, reason for studying French, academic aptitude, grade-point average, and foreign language grades.

Considering the complexity of the task undertaken by the second language learner, it is impressive that the subjects produced so many correct grammatical forms. However, for nearly every structure, between 20% and 70% of the responding subjects made an error of some kind. In addition, it must be remembered that those students who volunteered were statistically-significantly more able than those who declined the invitation, and that subjects further self-selected themselves by choosing the items for which they would ask questions. The percentage of error for each structure is, therefore, likely to be considerably higher in the general population of second-year French students. On the other hand, this sample of syntactical and morphological structures is a relatively small one, and, given an instrument with different vocabulary and structures, the results might lead to very different conclusions.

Errors in the corpus could generally be traced to one or both of these explanations: interference, both inter- and intralingual, and reduction. Some examples of relatively frequent errors which seem to be the result of interlingual interference are (1) the English word order in the interrogative *Est votre mère . . . ,* (2) the deletion of noun markers in *Buvez-vous vin ou café pour dîner?* , (3) the placement of the adjectives in *le français gouvernement* and *prochain été,* (4) the placement of the object pronoun in *le gouvernement* /āwwaye/ *vous,* and (5) what seem to be analogies based on the English interrogative "do" plus subject plus verb (e.g., *Quand faites-vous partir pour la France?*). Examples of relatively frequent errors that seem to be caused by intralingual interference are (1) *Combien des frères . . . ,* (2) *. . . plus grande de moi,* (3) *boivez* and *boirez,* (4) *le gouvernement de français,* and (5) *Est-ce que le gouvernement* /āwwaye/ *vous?*

Interference from English seemed to play a much larger and more general role than did interference from French. However, the greatest number, if not the widest variety, of errors seemed to be due to reduction.

The most widespread of these reductions was in tense markers. In sentences which were to be marked for tense or mood, the marker was reduced to the present indicative in at least 55% of the cases. (This is assuming that any marker except the present indicative or infinitive represented an attempt to produce the appropriate tense.) Another error, prevalent in items 5, 6, and 7 was the reduction of the number marker from second person plural to third person singular. Reduction from plural to singular forms was evident in at least half the cases for both the noun marker and the verb of item 3 (e.g., *Où est votre parent?*) and in a third of the sentences in item 2 which were based on the construction *Quels sont leurs noms?* Similarly, adjectives in item 4 were reduced to masculine forms in at least 60% of the cases.

The use of noun markers suggests a hierarchy:

Ø (no marker)
Definite article only
Features are distinguished:
   definite/indefinite
   masculine/feminine
   singular/plural
   possession

If the noun was marked in English, the noun was most often also marked correctly in French (except for gender) by the subjects, with a few occurrences of a simple definite article or ∅. If the noun was unmarked in English ("wine or coffee" and "with meals" and "on Sundays"), there were also large numbers of nouns unmarked in French, with another, smaller group of definite articles.

For 24% of the information-eliciting questions produced, the obligatory second interrogative signal was deleted, and the use of an inappropriate wh- word (who, what, etc.), which was a common error, implies the deletion of distribution requirements such as animate/inanimate.

There was some evidence for the relationship between some of these reductions and the complexity of the verbal element, but there seemed to be an additional factor operating here. If students were asked for *their* priorities in foreign language learning, it is doubtful that many would choose grammatical accuracy over communicational accuracy. (Reinert's survey, for example, revealed that "well over one-half of the students found speaking the most enjoyable aspect of their foreign language classes, and the learning of structures was the least popular."[2]) Several of the reductions that occurred in the language of the subjects in the present study seem to reflect this bias.

The verb was frequently deleted only in sentences containing stative verbs. In both sentences where a required plural marker was deleted, there was reason for the interlocutor to believe that Jacqueline knew how many people were involved in the question. The past tense in item 5 ("Where she was born") was attempted in many more cases than in item 6, where the temporal setting was fixed by the semantic content of the dependent clause ("... when she was a little girl"). The deletion of a required redundant interrogative signal (e.g., *Pourquoi vous ne parlez pas anglais?*), which was the most frequent error in the interrogative, did not result in a failure to communicate.

If correction of errors by the teacher results in a more adult grammar, it is possible that correction in terms of communication requirements might be more fruitful than any other kind, since this seems to be important to students. This, however, presents two problems—the normal classroom situation and the teacher himself. In the normal classroom situation "real" communication is rare. Stevick defines real language as that which occurs in a situation in which the interlocutor does not always know what answer he will receive.[3] While this is sometimes true of drill activity, slot substitution is obviously not natural language. Foreign language teachers, therefore, must strive to create more situations in which "real" communication, as defined here, can take place. The fact that so many students used inappropriate wh- words is a case in point. If they were encouraged to ask "real" questions, which rarely happens in a classroom, this might not be such a common error.

The teacher himself also presents a problem. Unfortunately, because few are native speakers of the foreign language they teach and because even those who are have learned to interpret their students' meanings, it is impossible for them to consistently make corrections in terms of the comprehensibility of the students' utterances to non-English-speaking natives. But there are some errors which would obviously make communication difficult if not impossible (e.g., interrogatives based on the English "do" plus subject plus verb construction), and others that would probably not impede comprehension (e.g., adjective agreement in most cases). At any rate, if students are going to choose structures in terms of communicational restrictions, it is imperative that they have realistic notions of what these are.

There are, in addition, a few errors which may be the result of pedagogical strategies. Confusion between the definite and indefinite noun markers may well be due to the failure of many teachers to make real distinctions during classroom presentations. Many introduce a mass noun with its definite marker (e.g., *Qu'est-ce que c'est? C'est l'argent.*), which is nonsense. The use of a part of *être* instead of *avoir* as the past tense auxiliary may be the result of introducing the two verbs and then turning immediately to idioms with *avoir,* such as *J'ai faim.* Similarly, that the grammatical nature of /apɛl/ should be misunderstood is not surprising when during the first few days of class students are often covertly urged to translate /apɛl/ as "name."

The series of chi-square tests was performed in order to determine if there was any evidence to support the contention that second language acquisition is comparable to first language acquisition in terms of its developmental nature. According to the mentalistic theories, any child of normal intelligence acquires his native language merely by being exposed to instances of it in use. His language acquisition device (LAD) processes this input and produces progressively sophisticated interim grammars which he uses in a systematic fashion.

It was assumed that the school the subject attended and his previous language experience would provide the linguistic data which his LAD would then process. Since there would not be considerable differences in ages between subjects, but considerable differences in proficiency were anticipated, it was hypothesized that the other five independent variables (willingness to persevere, reason for studying French, academic aptitude, grade point average, and foreign language grades) should reflect different developmental levels if a device such as LAD was actually functioning.

Unfortunately, specific errors did not occur frequently enough to permit the kind of analysis that was originally planned, and the majority of tests were performed using the categories "correct" and "incorrect" as the dependent variables.

There were 176 chi-square values significant at the .05 level or beyond, and the distribution of these significant values does not seem to present any kind of pattern except for four of the seven independent variables (school attended, academic aptitude, grade point average, and foreign language grades), where the highest number of significant results was 37. Although we cannot conclude that the failure of a chi-square test to reveal association between two variables means that no such association exists, the fact that there were so few significant values and that those which did appear did not do so consistently suggests that the independent variables selected are not representative of LAD, if such a construct exists.

However, attempts at tense markers and the specific kind of error made in the interrogative did not seem to be related to the school attended, while nearly all these features were related to the measures of academic success to some extent. The conclusion drawn from this was that those features whose appearance was associated with the school attended as well as measures of cognitive abilities are within the developmental range of many subjects, while those that were not associated with the school attended are beyond that range.

In any case, whether or not because of a "built-in syllabus" as Corder proposes,[4] there were many discernible patterns in the errors of these subjects.

If there is one conclusion to be drawn from the results of the present study, it is that we are trying to teach too much—too few students are successful in acquiring the syllabus we have proposed. The percentage of students who are successful in mastering the majority of the syllabus for active use is probably less than 10%. Belasco contends that trying to teach for *active* use the 40 to 50 grammar points normally included in a beginning text is futile and that a more practicable goal would be to teach the majority of these points for passive acquisition only and concentrate on a limited number of structures for active use.[5] Since the interrogative construction *est-ce que* appears to produce fewer errors, perhaps the inversion constructions ought to be taught only for passive control. It also appears that a radical reduction in the number of tenses presented is advisable. When many students are still having difficulty with person number agreement in the present tense after two years' study, it may be naive to try to tackle the intricacies of the imperfect.

Similarly, when the use of the partitive is rare, it seems absurd to try to teach its exceptions.

Because the subjects in the present study were volunteers and the corpus was so limited, the results can only be suggestive. Further research is needed to determine if the results are representative of other groups and of language produced in other situational contexts. There are many other related questions which also need examination. Would a reduced syllabus result in better learning of what was studied? How important is grammatical accuracy in communication with a non-English-speaking native, both in affective and cognitive terms? Would giving a student feedback on how his sentence might be interpreted by a native speaker lead to more correct utterances? The whole question of the effect of teacher correction on student learning has recently attracted much attention, and studies of first language acquisition suggest parallel questions in second language acquisition. Would correcting the student's invalid linguistic hypotheses result in a more advanced grammar of production? Are reductions more often the result of communication strategies made necessary by cognitive limits? If the latter is true, perhaps these should not be discouraged but rather guided by teacher responses which would reflect those that would be made by a native speaker. Perhaps, most of all, we need to reconsider our objectives: to what extent is it feasible in two years to prepare foreign language students for oral communication with native speakers?

NOTES

1. Albert Valdman, "Language Variation and the Teaching of French," in *Current Issues in Teaching French,* ed. Gaylord Todd (Philadelphia, Pa.: Center for Curriculum Development, 1972), p. 103.

2. Harry Reinert, "Student Attitudes toward FL–No Sale," *Modern Language Journal,* 54 (1970), 110.

3. Earl Stevick, "UHF and Microwaves in Transmitting Language Skills," *International Journal of American Linguistics,* 32 (1966), 87.

4. S.P. Corder, "The Significance of Learners' Errors," *International Review of Applied Linguistics,* 5 (1967), 165.

5. Simon Belasco, "The Relation of Linguistic Analysis to Foreign Language Teaching," in *Current Issues in Teaching French,* ed. Gaylord Todd (Philadelphia, Pa.: Center for Curriculum Development, 1972), p. 4.

2

TEACHING FOR COMMUNICATION

Sandra J. Savignon
University of Illinois

From *AATF National Bulletin,* vol. 2, no. 2 (November 1976).

Foreign language methodologists concerned with drawing the attention of the profession to the need for spontaneous, meaningful language use in the acquisition of a second language have made the distinction between *linguistic competence* and *communicative competence. Linguistic competence* may be defined as the mastery of the sound system and basic structural patterns of a language. *Communicative competence* may be defined as the ability to function in a truly communicative setting; that is, in a spontaneous transaction involving one or more other persons. As most experienced teachers will acknowledge, it is one thing to *know about* a language—verb forms, vocabulary items, basic grammatical patterns, and the like—and quite another to *know how* to use it effectively in a conversational exchange with a native speaker.

Imagine for a moment a student of French who has been asked out to dinner in a Paris restaurant or, to use an example on this side of the Atlantic, who has agreed to serve as an interpreter for a visitor from Rouen. The likelihood that any one of the phrases or expressions from his French I textbook will fit his particular situation is slim, if indeed he can even recall them! His chances of being served what he wants, or of giving the right information to the visitor, are much greater if he has learned *strategies* to cope with the linguistic disadvantage at which he inevitably finds himself:

What do I do when I don't understand?
What if I can't think of a word?
How can I overcome my embarrassment at not speaking fluently?
Self-assurance in real-life situations such as these comes not from repetition of patterned phrases but from *first,* understanding of what it means to communicate, and *second,* lots of practice in doing so.

The point is, all our students, no matter how long they study a second language, will find themselves eventually in the real world, outside the classroom, to discover they don't know "all" of French, or German, or Spanish, etc. They will have to make do with what they do know. How much better for them, whether they study a language for six years or six weeks, to have had the opportunity for spontaneous interaction in the classroom with their teacher's encouragement. How much better to have learned that it is unrealistic to expect to respond in perfectly pronounced patterns to completely understood requests. In any second-language learning there is much starting, stopping, repeating, and reflecting. Sounds are mispronounced; patterns are less than exact. What counts is getting the message across.

Most important to the learner's progress in developing communicative competence is a variety of activities in which the student can use the second language in unrehearsed, novel situations requiring, on his part, inventiveness, resourcefulness, and a good bit of aplomb. These are the activities which most closely approximate the real world of the second-language learner. They let him see just how well he could get along if certain situations came up. They let him measure his progress against criteria which he knows to be more real than weekly grammar quizzes or dialogue practice. Most importantly, perhaps, they let him experience for himself both the understandable apprehensions and increasing exhilarations of self-expression in another language. This experience will take him beyond verb forms and vocabulary lists—so easily forgotten as years go by—to more lasting insights into language and language use. With these insights he will better understand the special needs and feelings of all those persons in our society and abroad who seek to cross linguistic barriers.

You can help your students take the first step toward an understanding of second-language learning and at the same time prepare them for real-language activities by discussing with them the subject of communication in a second language. Have them think for a moment about exchanges they may have had with non-native speakers of English. How did they know they were talking to someone who had learned English as a second language? What kinds of "errors" did the person make—

pronunciation, vocabulary, or grammar? Did these non-standard forms interfere with meaning? Did some interfere more than others? What have been your students' emotional reactions to the non-native speech of persons they have known? Were they impatient at any difficulties they may have had in understanding? Or did they find the differences "quaint"? Or "amusing"? Have they had different kinds of feelings toward non-native speakers of different ethnic backgrounds? Was this due to the way they spoke or to feelings the students may have toward the ethnic group with which they identify a particular "accent"? Can they think of entertainers and other well-known persons who have a foreign accent? What is the effect? Do they think the accent may be deliberate in some cases for the impression it creates?

Your discussion should then go to a discovery of what is ultimately important in determining the success of an exchange. If they were trying to get some information from a Frenchman who knew only a little English, how would they want him to respond? If he didn't understand their question, would they want him to just stand there and shake his head? Or should he try to repeat, or ask them to repeat? Are there gestures or other forms of non-verbal communication that would be useful in helping them to get their meaning across?

You should then explain that real-language activities are concerned with just that—getting meaning across as effectively as they can, using every means at their disposal. They should not be overly concerned with completeness or the *mot juste.* Circumlocution is not only permitted, it is desirable if it furthers communication. Gestures will be useful. If they are not sure of a pronunciation, they should go ahead and try it anyway; maybe it will be understood. An English word with a French (Spanish, German, etc.) pronunciation may even get them by—there is, after all, *le tee-shirt, le stéréo!* In these real or simulated communicative setttings, it is *what* they say that counts, not *how* they say it.

"What!" some of you are surely responding to that last statement, "not be concerned with how they express themselves! Why, throughout my own professional preparation, I was always concerned with accuracy and propriety. And I hope to instill the same respect for the French language in my students. How can I permit them to say whatever they want and let it go uncorrected?"

Your reaction is understandable. Most of us who have been in the foreign language classroom within the last twenty years or so, whether as a student, teacher, or both, have learned to place great importance on linguistic accuracy. Beginning on a wide scale in the late 1950's proponents of the audio-lingual method stressed near-native speed and pronunciation in first-year students through the use of dialogue memorization and repetition of patterned responses. The number of phrases introduced was purposely limited with, again, the emphasis on accuracy. Above all, teachers were cautioned against moving too quickly lest the material not be "mastered." Under no circumstances were students to be allowed to express themselves in an area in which they had not had previous drilling. Truly spontaneous or creative language use was postponed until the later stages of language learning, typically the third or fourth years of high school study or later.

The intent was that students would reach a degree of familiarity with the materials presented which would then allow them to recombine patterns and vocabulary in a pseudo-communicative context (a sort of role playing modeled after the situation in a sample dialogue). In fact, however, most teachers never reached the recombination activities at the end of the unit. Conscious of having to complete a specified number of units by the end of the term, and concerned with student mastery of the basic material, there just did not seem to be time enough. Those teachers who did try to make time for students to use the patterns they had practiced in more authentic, true-to-life situations were in for a surprise. When put on their own, the majority of students simply could not readily use patterns and vocabulary spontaneously and fluently in a novel situation. There was much stumbling and hesitation, sometimes long and very complete silence. It is no wonder that a good many teachers found dialogue recitation to be a more convenient and face-saving way to test speaking ability![1]

The expectations created in the minds of both students and teachers by the audio-lingual method in its many variations have been essentially unrealistic. They have led to a good deal of disillusionment and discouragement. Teachers look upon "mistakes" in the speech of their students as a sign of failure, either on their part or their students'. Students are embarrassed or ashamed of their stumbling, anglicized utterances, expecting, rather, to be able to respond in complete sentences with near-native fluency.

Yet in looking back at their own experiences—as they were learning a second language, or subsequently in the front of the classroom—many teachers know that the first attempts to really express one's own ideas in a foreign language are accompanied by lots of false starts, groping for words, and outright blunders. It's the same whether you have studied a language for one year or five. Once on your own, it's a whole new ball game. These same teachers may also have noted that it is not always the "best" students who go on to perform well in an unstructured situation. They themselves may feel they know a lot about the language they teach and are very competent to present syntax, pronunciation, and vocabulary; but their self-assurance may vanish when confronted in a social situation with a real live native speaker.

In my own experiences with teaching and testing for communicative competence, I have found that students who were given the opportunity for innovative self-expression from the very beginning of their study of French far outperformed students who had not had the benefit of such experience in situations requiring spontaneous interaction with a native speaker. This in spite of the fact that both groups performed equally well on standardized tests of proficiency in French. The implications of these results are important. First, they suggest that the standardized tests on which we frequently base student grades or determine college placement are not a valid measure of a person's ability to use a foreign language in an authentic transaction. Second, it is apparent that innovative self-expression in which a student is encouraged to use creatively the language he is learning, regardless of errors, in no way decreases his linguistic accuracy.[2]

Of equal interest to foreign-language teachers along with student achievement is student attitude. All of us work best and stay longest in activities which give us a sense of accomplishment. The reactions of my beginning students to the opportunity for spontaneous use of French have been ones of enthusiasm and gratitude. Students frequently mention the confidence gained: "... the sessions especially gave me confidence in myself that I really could talk to someone in French"; "... I was able to get a better idea of how to express myself with limited vocabulary"; "These sessions taught me to say what I wanted to say instead of book conversations."

The comments of other beginning French students *not* involved in any systematic program to develop communicative skills offer further encouragement. Their reactions to a final examination requiring them to converse spontaneously with a native speaker indicate that these students, too, would welcome the opportunity to use French creatively throughout the term:

"I thought [the test] was fun, but very challenging. It doesn't seem as though we've had enough practice speaking off the top of our head. Until this evening, I was never forced to say anything except answers to questions or substitute phrases ... there was no need to search for words ... they were supplied. I wish we were forced to do this more often. This is what a language should be."

"It seems very difficult, but it is the first time I have had the chance to actually express myself in French ... I feel I have an 'A' in French 101 writing, reading, and grammar, but an 'E' [failure] in actually having a practical knowledge of the language."

"If this is an easy test, I just found that I couldn't talk my way out of the airport if I flew to France."

There are a variety of classroom activities which not only encourage but *require* spontaneous language use in the classroom. Role playing, discussion topics, and games all represent strategies for providing the emotional involvement necessary for authentic interaction in the classroom. Not all activities are suited to all students at all times. Some students, the natural actors, will particularly enjoy the role playing. Encourage them to create their own scenarios. (These should be unrehearsed, *commedia dell'arte* type sketches, *not memorized dialogue.*) Others will prefer small group discussion where there is no pressure on a particular person to speak at any one time. Try to respect individual differences as much as you can. Let each student find a sense of achievement in whatever kinds of language activities he enjoys most.

As they begin the role playing, games, and other activities, many of your students will be naturally shy. Many of them are ill at ease performing extemporaneously in English, let alone in a second language. You can help enormously by (1) not criticizing their efforts, and (2) relating to them in as friendly, authentic a manner as possible. This is not the time to correct grammar or to ask for complete sentences. Try, just for the moment, to forget you are a language teacher and to listen instead as an interested participant. If you don't understand a statement addressed to you, let the other person know. Ask him to repeat or to explain, if he can. Or you can restate what you thought you understood for his confirmation. Be helpful, be honest, but never hurtful.

Students will want to say things for which they have not yet learned the words. Encourage them to ask you for the words they need. The best time to learn a new word is when you really want to know it. You are not expected to know every word either, of course. If someone wants to talk about threshing machines, and you have never spent any time on a mechanized farm in a country where the language is spoken, chances are you will have to look it up. If there is no time for that at the moment, call it "threshing machine" and try to describe it so a foreign speaker could understand.

There are lots of words and expressions that you can give your students to help them save face on those numerous occasions when they can't think of a word or need time to collect their thoughts. There may be second-language equivalents of "thing," "whatchamacallit," etc., which can fill in for just about any concrete noun. *How do you say . . . , Will you please repeat . . . , I'm sorry, I didn't understand . . .* are necessary phrases to have in your repertoire if you are to let a fast-speaking native know just how much he is getting across. Equivalents for *let's see* . . . , *I mean* . . . , *um* . . . and other such expressions serve to keep the conversation going while you pause to get your bearings.

A single gesture sometimes says more than a thousand words. Show your students the typical gestures you know and use them yourself. Handshaking, shoulder shrugging, fist waving, and lip pursing all have their place and are fun to learn.

Exploit the resources of your community to create the occasion for authentic communications. Perhaps there is a visiting exchange student living nearby. There may be professional people who would enjoy coming to the school to talk with students. You need not be concerned that their accent is unfamiliar or their language too advanced. Let your students handle the situation as best they can. The more authentic the better.

Explore the possibility of small group activities that bring together students from different levels of language study. Many games and discussions are more fun a second and third time with different participants. The more advanced students can serve as resource persons when you are not there; and the satisfaction they will gain from explaining something to someone else is important to their own motivation for continued study.

Don't overlook the contributions technology can make to communication. Local radio and television programs in the second language exist in many communities. If not in yours, have you thought about using a short-wave radio? More and more schools are successfully incorporating broadcasts from other countries into their programs. They offer up-to-date commentary on a variety of topics in language that is fresh and real. Some teachers with a ham radio operator's license let their students transmit in the language to points around the United States and Canada.[3]

The telephone is a readily accessible means for providing additional occasions for conversation. You might want to set up a system of "phone pals" whereby students exchange messages with each other or with native speakers in the community. You could conduct a telephone clinic one hour a week in which you answer any questions put to you in the second language including, as an incentive, questions on the content of the next day's quiz.

Learn to relax about your own "errors." Unless you are a native speaker, chances are you make them. Don't let that keep you from talking spontaneously with your students. You will get better with practice, and more importantly, you will be allowing them the practice *they* need to improve. Don't be afraid to admit it when you don't know a word or pronunciation. Your frank admission of what you do and don't know will make you that much more credible in the eyes of your students. It will ultimately serve to give your students confidence that they, too, can learn the language.

Use the first five minutes or so of every class period to talk with your students in the second language about things of interest to them. The things they talk about spontaneously among themselves before the bell rings are a good clue as to what really interests them. If you, too, chat with them in English before the bell, try to continue the same conversation in the second language. This has the advantage of giving you a topic to discuss on which you've already had some warm-up. Ideas have been expressed, differing points of view noted or perhaps an amusing or dramatic anecdote begun.

Use the second language to talk to your students about the things that concern you all in the day-to-day classroom routine. Discussions of assignments, corrections, class activities, and so forth constitute the most natural opportunity available for authentic communication. Make the most of it.

Finally, do everything you can to get to know your students as individuals, with lives and concerns that extend far beyond the four walls of the language classroom. You might ask them to fill out a three-by-five card at the beginning of the term indicating their special interests, any jobs they may hold, musical instruments they play, and other talents. This information will give you a headstart in helping to make class activities more meaningful to all of you.

Once you and your students begin to use real-language activities and to understand their value, you will no doubt find contexts which have particular meaning for you, your class, and your community. Above all, remember that for it to be real, communication must be a personalized, spontaneous event. It cannot be programmed. Only you can make it happen.

NOTES

(This paper was delivered at a plenary session of the Fourth International Conference of the Ontario Modern Language Teachers Association and the New York State Association of Foreign Language Teachers, Toronto, February 28, 1975. It modifies slightly an earlier article, "Teaching for Communication," in R. Coulombe, J.C. Barré, C. Fostle, N. Paulin, S.J. Savignon, *Voix et Visages de la France: Level I,* Teacher's Edition, Chicago: Rand McNally & Co., 1974, pp.

T13-20. Readers interested in applications for French may refer to the real-language activities included in this text. A Spanish edition with similar applications is forthcoming.)

1. In one survey of methods of testing speaking skill at the high school level, 93 per cent of the teachers questioned reported basing their evaluations primarily on the recitation of memorized dialogues. For a complete report, see Theodore B. Kalivoda, "Oral Testing in Secondary Schools," *Modern Language Journal*, 54 (May 1970).

2. The research referred to here, along with the students' comments quoted below, is described fully in my book, *Communicative Competence: An Experiment in Foreign-Language Teaching*, Montreal: Marcel Didier, Ltée., 1972. This volume includes a detailed account of the teaching and testing procedures I established as well as a statistical analysis of the results of an experiment I conducted at the University of Illinois at Urbana-Champaign.

3. For an introduction to the use of radio in the modern language classroom, see Robert J. Nelson and Richard E. Wood, "Radio in Foreign Language Education," ERIC/CAL Series in Applied Linguistics, Arlington, VA: Center for Applied Linguistics, 1975.

$$\textbf{3}$$

STRUCTURAL PATTERN DRILLS:
A CLASSIFICATION

Christina Bratt Paulston
University of Pittsburgh

From *Foreign Language Annals,* vol. 4, no. 2 (December 1970), pp. 187-193.

The basic core of the audiolingual method of teaching foreign languages is drills: pronunciation drills, vocabulary drills, but most of all structural pattern drills. This emphasis on drills reflects the beliefs about the nature of language and of learning by the advocates of this method. Wilga Rivers has examined these assumptions and a quick glance at the table of contents tells us what they are:[1]

1. Foreign-language learning is basically a mechanical process of habit formation. Corollary 1: Habits are strengthened by reinforcement. Corollary 2: Foreign-language habits are formed most effectively by giving the right response, not by making mistakes. Corollary 3: Language is behavior and behavior can be learned only by inducing the student to behave.
2. Language skills are learned more effectively if items of the foreign language are presented in spoken form before written.

3. Analogy provides a better foundation for foreign language learning than analysis.

Small wonder then that drills are emphasized in the classroom. By what other method could one teach a set of spoken habits by inducing the students into active habit formation with a minimum opportunity for error? Indeed, one might wonder how people learned languages before the audiolingual method.

The plethora of various types of drills is overwhelming. To give but a few examples, Brooks lists twelve types: repetition, inflection, replacement, restatement, completion, transposition, expansion, contraction, transformation, integration, rejoinder, and restoration.[2] Finocchiaro describes eleven pattern practice activities under their "commonly agreed upon names": substitution, replacement, paired sentences, transformation or conversion, expansion, reduction, directed practice, integration, progressive replacement, translation, and question-answer.[3] Dacanay claims that there are basically four kinds of drill activity: substitution, transformation, response, and translation, but with a variety of subtypes which are: simple substitution, correlative substitution, moving slot substitution, transposition, expansion, transposition with expansion, reduction, integration, integration with transposition and reduction, comprehension check-up, short answer, short rejoinder, choice questions, patterned response, and five types of translation drills.[4] The criteria in classifying drills into these typologies are primarily in terms of what Frank Johnson has named the "restructuring range" and the "amount range." The restructuring range indicates the type of restructuring of a cue and the complexity of this restructuring which a learner must go through to arrive at a response. The amount range indicates how much information a learner is expected to retain and reproduce in giving a response.[5] The major drawback with these typologies is that they do not provide a method of gradation of drills even though gradation of language teaching materials is considered one of the most important aspects of the audiolingual method.

Furthermore, these assumptions of language learning on which drills are based have been challenged by the transformation-generative grammarians[6] who believe that language learning involves internalizing a complex system of rules—by innate propensities for language acquisition—which will generate all and only the grammatical sentences of a language. T-G grammatical theory distinguishes between competence, the intuitive knowledge of this complex system of rules, and performance, the actual utterance. "Acceptable performance is not possible while competence is defective. Practice in performance in the classroom is practice in generating new utterances, not in parroting utterances produced by the teacher."[7]

At this point I would like to propose a theoretical classification of structural pattern drills which attempts to incorporate both the theories of Chomsky and Skinner.[8] The proposal does not contain any new data, but rather reinterprets old data in light of new theory in order to provide a more efficient working model for the classroom.[9]

When one talks about language learning, one really is talking about the concatenation of two separate areas, the system of language and the process of learning. Rivers, reviewing the writings of Skinner, Osgood, Chomsky, Lashley and Miller, Galanter and Pribram, points out that they all seem to agree that there are probably at least two levels of language: mechanical skill and thought.[10] These levels seem to correlate with what Katona has found in his experiments on learning by two methods: a "direct practice" and a "method of understanding" or as Rivers rephrases "a mechanical level and a level which involves understanding of how one is learning and the essential elements of what is being learned."[11]

If language involves more than one level and there are two types of learning, then this should be reflected in the nature and use of drills. In fact, with the judicious use of drills, we should find the answer to the constant plaint of the language teacher: "How can I make my students express their own ideas, using those language patterns they have memorized so laboriously?"

My contention is this. Given the plethora of different kinds of drills, we could use these drills more efficiently in our teaching if we analyzed them in terms of (1) expected terminal behavior, (2) of response control, (3) of the type of learning process involved, and (4) of utterance response. I suggest that basically there are three classes of drills: mechanical, meaningful, and communicative. There is no such thing as a more meaningful drill; either a drill is meaningful or it is not. However, there are gray areas between the classes, and they are of two kinds. One is a mixed drill where the cue in a chain-drill or a three-step drill may be mechanical and the response meaningful, and the other where a knowledge of the structural class (as in a moving slot substitution drill) may be sufficient.

A mechanical drill is defined as a drill where there is complete control of the response, where there is only one correct way of responding. Because of the *complete* control, the student need not even understand the drill nor necessarily pay attention to what he is doing. The most extreme example of this type of drill is repetition and mim-mem. Substitution drills lend themselves particularly well to this:

	+	3	+
Example:	Pɔɔm	nakrian	Pɔɔm
	+	3	+
	suuŋ:	nakrian	suuŋ
	2	3	2
	ʔuan:	nakrian	ʔuan

Continue the drill:

+
1. naaw

3
2. rɔɔn

3. dii

2
4. suay[12]

I don't know how many readers know Thai, but I do know that you could all successfully complete the drill. There is complete control of the response.

The expected terminal behavior of such drills is the automatic use of manipulative patterns and is commensurate with the assumption that language learning is habit formation. It involves the classical Skinnerian method of learning through instrumental conditioning by immediate reinforcement of the right response. Learning takes place through analogy and allows transfer of identical patterns. This is clearly the mechnical level of learning, and this class of drills provides practice in mechanical associations such as adjective-noun agreement, verb endings, question-forms and the like. This is a very necessary step in language learning, and as long as the student is learning, he won't mind the mechanical nature of the drill. The teacher needs to remember that the student can drill without understanding and to make sure that in fact he does understand. Because of the response-control, it is eminently suited for choral drills.

However, much of the criticism against the audiolingual method is based on the mechanical drill or rather on the overuse to which it has been put. Drilled beyond mastery of the pattern, it induces tedium and a distaste for language learning.[13] Lambert points out that motivation is one of the prime factors in successful language learning, and we simply cannot afford student distaste.[14] Furthermore, "it has been demonstrated that there is a limit to the amount of repetition which is effective for language learning,"[15] i.e., overuse of mechanical drills is not efficient teaching.

While not denying the need for mechanical drills, we may note that on the mechanical level alone, the student certainly cannot yet express his own ideas fluently. He now needs to work through a set of meaningful drills:

Association/Fixed reply[16]

1. Teacher: for five years
   Student: How long did he (study)?

2. Teacher: during March
   Student: When did he (register)?

3. Teacher: until four o'clock
   Student:

In a meaningful drill there is still control of the response (although it may be correctly expressed in more than one way and as such is less suitable for choral drilling), but the student cannot complete the drill without fully understanding structurally and semantically what he is saying. You might say there is a built-in test design. There is a choice involved in his answer, and the criterion he uses in answering is often given to him; the class supplies him with the information. Comprehension-type questions and answers based on assigned readings fall in this class.

Teacher: What time did John come to school?
Student: John came to school at 9 o'clock.

as well as much "situational" teaching:

Where is the book?
It's on the table.
Where is the chalk?
It's in the box.

If the teacher is unsure of whether a drill is mechanical or meaningful (the borders are not completely clear), he can test it with a nonsense word.

Example:
           I walk to school every day.
Cue: run
Response: I run to school every day.

Teacher: skip
Student: I skip to school every day.

Teacher:	summersault
Student:	I summersault to school every day.

Teacher:	boing
Student:	I boing to school every day.

Now do the same drill in Thai:

Example:

$$+ \qquad\qquad\qquad 3$$

Can dəən pay roŋrian Tuk wan

Cue: wiŋ

Response: $+ \quad 2 \qquad\qquad 3$

Can wiŋ pay roŋrian Tuk wan

| |

Teacher: kradoot

$+ \quad | \; | \qquad\qquad 3$

Student: Can kradoot pay roŋrian Tuk wan

Teacher: tii laŋ kaa

$+ \qquad\qquad\qquad 3$

Student: Can tii laŋ kaa pay roŋrian Tuk wan

Teacher: boing

$+ \qquad\qquad 3$

Student: Can boing pay roŋrian Tuk wan[17]

Those are mechanical drills. But in the drill on prepositions above, no native speaker could ever answer "Where boings the book?" for the simple reason that he does not understand it. It is a meaningful drill. Complexity of pattern is not an issue.

Example:

        John kicked the door.

        The door was kicked by John.

Cue: The dog bit the man.

        The boing boinged the boing.

Response: The man was bitten by the dog.

        The boing was boinged by the boing.

That is a mechanical drill. For the language teacher who is fluent in the target language, it is difficult to appreciate the enormous difference in difficulty by these two classes of drills. This is not to deny that a response like "The man was bitten by the dog," albeit in a mechanical drill, is much more difficult for the learner than a single lexeme substitution drill. Language learning is also the ability to control increasing amounts of language in mechanical manipulation and we need to consider the difficulty level within the "amount range" as well.

A word of caution. Sometimes a drill will seem meaningful when it really isn't.

Teacher: Holds up a book
Student 1:   What is this?
Student 2:   It is a book.

Meaningful or mechanical? It depends on what you are teaching. If you are teaching the structural patterns: Question word/thing + be + demonstrative pronoun/thing and personal/thing + be + Np, it is one of the mixed class drills I mentioned earlier. Student 1 does not have to understand anything as long as he says "What's this?" Student 2 has to understand in order to answer. However, this may be a vocabulary drill (we surely don't teach structural patterns and vocabulary at the same time) and that easily confuses the classification of the drills. Vocabulary by definition has lexical meaning and so does not fit into this classification of structural pattern drills.

It will be noticed that in the meaningful Q-A drills above the long answers were given. The expected terminal behavior has not changed. We still want an automatic use of language manipulations; we are still working on habit formation. But the method is different. The drill should be preceded by analysis of the characteristics of the language pattern—be it inductively coaxed out of the students or explained by the teacher. Unless the student understands what he is doing, i.e., recognizes the characteristic features involved in the language manipulation, he cannot complete the drill. There still is a right response (we have supplied facts and information), but we allow a bit of trial-and-error process in finding it.

But there is still no real communication taking place. Students have a tendency to learn what they are taught rather than what we think we are teaching. If we want to acquire fluency in expressing their own opinions, then we have to teach that. The expected terminal behavior in communicative drills is normal speech for communication or, if one prefers, the free transfer of learned language patterns to appropriate situations.

In a communicative drill there is no control of the response. The student has free choice of answer, and the criterion of selection here is his own opinion of the real world—whatever he wants to say. Whatever control there is lies in the stimulus. "What did you have for breakfast?"

is likely to limit the topic to the edible world but not necessarily. "I overslept and skipped breakfast so I wouldn't miss the bus" is an answer I have heard more than once. It still remains a drill rather than free communication because we are still within the realm of the cue-response pattern. Communication "requires interpersonal responsiveness, rather than the mere production of language which is truthful, honest, accurate, stylistically pleasing, etc.—those characteristics which look at language as language rather than as behavior, which is the social purpose of language. Our end product is surely getting things done, easing social tensions, goading ourselves into doing this or that, and persuading others to do things. Communication arises when language is used as such interpersonal behavior, which goes beyond meaningful and truthful manipulation of language symbols."[18] To recapitulate, the differences between a meaningful drill and a mechanical drill lie in the expected terminal behavior (automatic use of language manipulation versus free transfer of learned language patterns to appropriate situations) and in response control. But the main difference between a meaningful drill and a communicative drill is that the latter adds *new* information about the *real* world. All of us have seen a meaningful drill turn communicative when the students suddenly took the question or cue personally and told us something about himself that we did not know from the classroom situation. "I have three sisters" is communicative, but "My shirt is red" is merely meaningful; that information is supplied by the situation, and I can see it as well as the student.

Language teachers have always used communicative drills in the classroom (where else is one asked such personal questions as "Did you brush your teeth this morning?"), but my point is that there should be an orderly progress from mechanical drilling through meaningful to communicative drills, that the teacher should know one from the other, and that one should not rely on chance that the students will turn a drill into communication.

Communicative drills are the most difficult to arrange within the classroom. They can of course never be drilled chorally. Still, if we want fluency in expressing personal opinion, we have to teach that. One way of working with communicative drills is to structure the classroom activity so that it eliminates the outside world of the students and to work within this situation. Need I point out that running through a memorized dialogue with accompanying gestures and action is not communicative drill nor necessarily language learning; non-language teachers refer to such activity as acting. Another, simpler way of working with communicative drills is simply to instruct students to answer truthfully.

Example:

1. What is your responsibility?

    My responsibility is $\begin{cases} \text{to (learn English).} \\ \text{(learning English).} \end{cases}$

2. What's your hobby?

    My hobby is $\begin{cases} \text{to (make models).} \\ \text{(making models).} \end{cases}$

3. What's your favorite pastime?
4. What are your lab instructions?
5. What will your occupation be?
6. What are your interests?
7. What is your advice to (Ahmed)?[19]

Gone is the instrumental conditioning; there is no facilitating of the correct response. What we have is John Carroll's " 'problem-solving' situation in which the student must find . . . appropriate verbal responses for solving the problem, 'learning' by a trial-and-error process, to *communicate* rather than merely to utter the speech patterns in the lesson plan."[20] We are clearly working within a level of language that involves thought and opinion and teaching it in a way that necessitates an understanding of the essential elements of what is being learned. It is a very different experience from mechanical drilling. It is indeed practice in performance by practice in generating new utterances, and if it is indeed true that this is the only type of practice in performance, then it is also the only way of internalizing the rules of grammar so that competence will not be defective. I am not saying that language teaching should be concerned solely with communicative type drills, but I am suggesting that any amount of mechanical drills will not lead to competence in a language, i.e., fluency to express one's own opinions in appropriate situations.

To summarize, in language teaching we ought to classify the drills we use into three classes: mechanical, meaningful, and communicative in order to reach free communication. We then need to proceed systematically, not leaving out any one step. Mechanical drills are especially necessary in beginning courses and in learning languages markedly different from the native tongue, such as Thai is for me. I do not believe that this is the only way of teaching languages because it patently is not. Rather, given what we know about languages and learning today, this classification of drills will provide for more efficient language learning.

The limitation of this classification is that it only fits structural pattern drills. By definition, vocabulary involves meaning and thus cannot exist on a mechanical level only. Pronunciation drills are frequently carried out in nonsense syllables in order to concentrate the better on sounds; pronunciation of segmental phonemes does not involve meaningful utterances.

NOTES

1. Wilga M. Rivers, *The Psychologist and the Foreign Language Teacher* (Chicago: Univ. of Chicago Press, 1964), pp. vii-viii.

2. Nelson Brooks, *Language and Language Learning* (New York: Harcourt, 1964), p. 156.

3. Mary Finocchiaro, *English as a Second Language: From Theory to Practice* (New York: Regents, 1964), pp. 60-65.

4. Fe R. Dacanay, *Techniques and Procedures in Second Language Teaching* (Dobbs Ferry, N.Y.: Oceana, 1963),, pp. 107-151.

5. Dr. Francis C. Johnson, Professor of English, Univ. of Papua and New Guinea. In personal communication, July 31, 1970. I am for once in complete concord with his observations and very grateful to him for having made them.

6. For a succinct discussion, which reviews the literature and sums up the major points, see Wilga M. Rivers, *Teaching Foreign Language Skills* (Chicago: Univ. of Chicago Press, 1968), pp. 64-67.

7. Rivers summarizing the implications for foreign language teaching based on T-G principles. *Teaching Foreign Language Skills,* p. 67.

8. I want to express my gratitude to my students in "Techniques and Procedures in TESOL," especially Mary Newton Bruder, Walter Davison, and Frank Giannotta for their contribution to the development of the classification and the zeal with which they have tested it in their teaching. Whatever inadequacies remain are entirely my own.

9. See, e.g., Brooks, *Language Learning.*

10. *The Psychologist and the Foreign Language Teacher,* p. 47. Not to be confused with structural versus semantic meaning.

11. *The Psychologist and the Foreign Language Teacher,* p. 50.

12. Edward M. Anthony et al., *Foundations of Thai—Book 1, Part 1* (Pittsburgh: Univ. of Pittsburgh, 1967), p. 31.

This drill in translation runs like this:

Example (by teacher):

Cue: thin   Response: the thin student
      tall   the tall student
      fat   the fat student

Continue the drill:

Cue (by teacher):   Response (by student):
      cold   the cold student
      hot   the hot student
      good   the good student
      pretty   the pretty student

13. An operational definition of mastery of a pattern at this level might be when a student can run through a drill without paying attention to what he is

saying. To illustrate, I remember sitting by the window watching the futile efforts of a policeman to control Lima traffic, thinking about the menu for tomorrow's party, all the while loudly and clearly running through Spanish verb endings. The dinner was a success, but I certainly was not learning any Spanish.

14. Wallace E. Lambert, "Psychological Approaches to the Study of Language," *Modern Language Journal,* 47 (1963), 51-62, 114-121.

15. Rivers, *The Psychologist and the Foreign Language Teacher,* p. 151.

16. William E. Rutherford, *Modern English: A Textbook for Foreign Students* (New York: Harcourt, 1968), p. 234.

17. Miss Patamaka Patamapongse translated this drill.

18. Johnson, personal communication, July 31, 1970.

19. Rutherford, *Modern English,* p. 175. The teaching point here is using the complement to V_t + O (as in *to learn English*) in free variation with V + ing + O (as in *learning English*). The teacher asks the questions and the students answer.

20. John B. Carroll, *The Study of Language* (Cambridge, Mass.: Harvard Univ. Press, 1953), p. 188.

INTERACTION ACTIVITIES
IN THE FOREIGN CLASSROOM,
OR HOW TO GROW A TULIP-ROSE

Christina Bratt Paulston *and* Howard R. Selekman
University of Pittsburgh

From *Foreign Language Annals,* vol. 9, no. 3 (May 1976), pp. 248-254.

This paper reports on a project using a foreign language for free communication in a beginning language class. The original impetus for the project was found in two articles, one by Wilga Rivers[1] and one by Christina Bratt Paulston.[2] The first part of the paper outlines the conceptual framework; the second reports on classroom procedures and techniques.

There are many indications that standard audiolingual theory in foreign language teaching is outmoded. We deliberately use such a word for, in many cases, it seems that we are merely exchanging one set of assumptions for another without much empirical evidence. Some of the more extravagant claims of the cognitive codists accurately reflect the current fashions in linguistics, but evidence to support these claims is still lacking. In these days of claims and counterclaims in the foreign language teaching field, we might do well to look for areas of consensus.

There is increasing change from an emphasis on teaching to an emphasis on the learning situation, along with interest in individualized instruction and a recognition that learning strategies vary with individuals. There seems to be a general, if vague, agreement that exclusively teacher-centered learning is not the most efficient way to teach. No one argues with Wallace Lambert's findings that one of the most basic factors in language learning is motivation.[3] The conclusion for the classroom teacher should be simple: it would make sense to structure the situation so that the student learns through meaningful communication with his peers in a situation he enjoys. As we say in Swedish, it is simple enough to say "tulip-rose," but another matter to grow one.

The unstated assumption is that our objectives in language teaching have not changed; we are still mainly concerned with giving our students linguistic and communicative competence in a foreign language, knowing when to say what to whom in a comprehensible manner. Reading courses, translation courses, *explication de texte* courses have valid objectives, but it is only through a clear focus on our objectives that we can evaluate the results of our teaching.

Many of our students read and translate quite well, but when it comes to talking French or German or Spanish they are worse than hesitant, they are tongue-tied and embarrassed. As Rivers points out, we still have not come to grips with our basic problem: how to develop communicative ability, how to engineer the great leap to an autonomous stage of language use.[4] Perhaps communicative language use cannot be taught, but it most certainly can be learned—and opportunities for such learning should become routine in the language classroom.

No student sprang fully-Spanish-speaking from his teacher's forehead, and one cannot deny the crucial necessity for acquiring language skills before using them (skill-getting and skill-using in Rivers' model).[5] Nor can one acquire sufficient skills to communicate in a language if these skills are never used for communication. Thus, the problem becomes one of carefully sequencing learning activities from mechanical mastery of linguistic forms to communicative interaction in language. Sandra Savignon's study[6] points out that students can be quite patient during the form-acquiring stage if they know that they can soon use these forms for a practical purpose.

There are four stages in this process from mechanical learning to free communication: mechanical drills, meaningful drills, communicative drills, and communicative interaction. Two points need to be stressed. Each pattern should be taken through the sequence of all three classes of drills and, if possible, then used in a communicative interaction activity. Often, however, there is no control of language patterns in the communication activity, as the students use the patterns they need and know. Some may object that this is not possible within the time available. It is, if one eliminates the many mechanical drills students are asked to parrot, and instead substitutes meaningful and communicative drills.

The other point is that communicative drills should be present in the classroom within the first week of a beginning course and communication activities not later than the third week. As Rivers puts it, "Where we have been failing may well be in not encouraging this 'adventurous spirit' from an early stage, with the result that the student finds it difficult to move from structured security to the insecurity of reliance on his own resources. . . ."[7] Indeed, with our emphasis on immediate reinforcement of correct response, we may have carefully trained students not to make any response at all unless they know it to be correct.

STAGE 1: MECHANICAL DRILLS[8]

These are the drills which form the core of audiolingual textbooks and which have led to the severe (and justified) criticism of this approach. A mechanical drill is a drill in which there is complete control of the response and only one correct way of responding. The ability to practice mechanical drills without necessarily understanding them is an important criterion in distinguishing them from meaningful drills: if a nonsense word can be inserted by the student as a meaningful word, the drill is mechanical. A drill that can be done chorally is probably mechanical.

These drills are necessary in the beginning and intermediate stages of language learning in order to memorize patterns and achieve automatic use of manipulative patterns, i.e., they provide practice in mechanical associations such as adjective-noun agreement, verb endings, etc. They are done rapidly; a ten-item drill should take about seventy seconds. Three drills are usually sufficient for a pattern of average difficulty and are best done chorally to ensure maximum participation.

Example of Mechanical Drills[9]

Teacher:	Student:
Carlos is studying.	What is Carlos studying?
Bill is eating.	What is Bill eating?
The boys are playing.	What are the boys playing?
The women are cooking.	What are the women cooking?

STAGE 2: MEANINGFUL DRILLS

The expected terminal behavior remains the same as in mechanical drills: automatic use of manipulative patterns. However, the student cannot complete these drills without understanding what he is saying structurally and semantically. There is still control of the response, although it may be expressed in more than one way; there is a right answer, and the student is supplied with the information necessary for responding, either by the teacher, the classroom situation, or the assigned reading. Comprehension-type questions and answers based on assigned readings are in this class of drills. Here is a meaningful drill on the same teaching point as the mechanical drill above:[10]

Teacher:	Someone is eating.
Student #1:	Who is eating?
Student #2:	(Bill) is eating.
S1:	What is Bill eating?
S2:	Bill is eating (an apple).
T:	Some people are studying.
S1:	Who is studying?
S2:	(Jane) and (Bob) are studying.
S1:	What are they studying?
S2:	They're studying (American politics).

These drills should be done individually or, where possible, in small groups or pairs. They should be preceded by a grammatical explanation, and the students should be corrected when they make mistakes. These drills often sound halting after a set of mechanical drills since they are much more difficult for the student.

STAGE 3: COMMUNICATIVE DRILLS

The objective is normal speech for communication, and we must insist on comprehensible speech. The control is very loose, and the student can say whatever he wants; however, the drill is designed to elicit the pattern the class is working on. The difference between this class of drills and the others is that the student now supplies new information; he tells us about himself, what he did or what he thinks. Whatever the answer, the teacher cannot anticipate it.

These drills are time-consuming, and the students fumble and hesitate in a problem-solving approach to language learning, but they are developing communicative ability and enjoying it. Only errors which lead to miscomprehension should be corrected; the student needs encouragement to express himself, and nothing is less encouraging than constant correction of mistakes when the student is concentrating on his message. This is not yet communication, because we are still within the realm of the cue-response pattern. Here is an example of a communicative drill:[11]

T: Ask (Jane) what she's doing.

S1:   What are you doing?

S2:   I'm (studying English).

T: Ask (Bill) what he's reading.

S1:   What are you reading?

S2:   I'm reading (a novel).

It is the next step which is most difficult, the leap into autonomous language use.

STAGE 4: INTERACTION ACTIVITY

"We must work out situations, from an early stage, where the student is on his own, trying to use the language for the normal purpose of language: establishing social relations, seeking and giving information, expressing his reactions, learning to do something, hiding his intentions or talking his way out of trouble, persuading, discouraging, entertaining others, or displaying his achievements."[12] Here is our tulip-rose: a situation so structured that the student learns primarily from his peers and has a good time doing it.

These activities tend to be noisy, but the teacher need not be alarmed if his supervisor is not. The students concentrate so hard on their task that they block out surrounding noise. The noise, in fact, attests that language is being used for purposeful communication. Any form of communication is acceptable—gestures, drawings, pantomime, as well as language. The use of the student's native language may get out of hand in beginning classes, but Savignon reports favorably on it; her students learned the phrase very early *Comment dit-on 'x' en français?* This practice tends to limit the native language to isolated vocabulary items, and it teaches the students to talk themselves out of trouble. Vocabulary learned through immediate need tends to be well retained.

Grammar and pronunciation errors should be both expected and ignored, as long as they do not interfere with meaning. The point here, as Rivers points out, is innovation and experimentation with the new language, and constant correction is not conducive to experimentation. If the teacher wishes, he can keep lists of repetitive errors and discuss them later with individual students.

What follows is an account of a series of communicative interaction activities. While acclaim for communicative activities abounds on the theoretical level, there is as yet little in the literature on the technique level which systematically attempts to incorporate implications from theory into classroom behavior. The following is an attempt to do so.

BACKGROUND

These interaction activities were introduced in the religious school of a synagogue in Pittsburgh. The sole purpose of Judaic instruction in this school was to preserve and transmit heritage by giving students experiences and practice with congregational, liturgical skills. Recently, an audiolingual program in Hebrew was introduced. The text is quite similar to early audiolingual materials. It contains many drills, most of them mechanical, and has many dialogues to be memorized; pattern presentations often introduce three or four grammatical items simultaneously. Attempts at even pseudo-communication are minute and ill-sequenced in the course of activities, and no communication approaching true interaction is offered until the second level.

The students are twelve and thirteen years of age and attend Hebrew school three times a week. Weekday sessions occur after a full day of public school. They arrive exhausted and are expected to extend their attention span for another two hours. Student interest, for the most part, is minimal; the sole motivation is that attendance is a prerequisite for the Bar/Bat Mitzvah. Many parents have also told their children that whatever they do in Hebrew school is secondary and less important than their work in public school. Mechanical drilling was no solution to the problems, but the introduction of some honest communicative interaction proved invaluable.

SUPER SPY

This game of interaction has been enormously successful with students, for it is loud, alive, cooperative, competitive, and fun. Students are divided into groups of four or five. Each student in each group has a chance to be a "spy." Each round of the game consists of the following:

(1) The spies from each team go outside the room as a group and decide on a secret mission. The first time we played, we had been studying Hebrew expressions for "to have to do something." The spy group was controlled to the extent that their mission had to be expressed in the "to have to do something" format. Many times the spy group has not been given any guidelines. An example of a secret mission is, "I have to go to the store to buy things for the Sabbath tomorrow." Each spy tests the others to make sure that all spies are sure of the mission and can verbalize the mission in Hebrew.

(2) The spies return to their respective groups, and the groups compete to try to learn the mission from the spy following certain ground rules:

(a) A word of English disqualifies the team;
(b) A ban on asking in Hebrew, "What are you supposed to do?"
Problem solving is an important aspect of this activity. If students found themselves at a loss to express themselves in Hebrew, they could use charades or drawings.

(3) The first team to decode the mission shouts out some appropriate Hebrew expression indicating their success. All teams stop working while a representative from the team—not the spy—verbalizes the mission in Hebrew. If the representative is incorrect, the other teams get two more minutes to try and determine the mission. If at the end of the two minutes, no one has the correct answer, the spies reveal the mission in Hebrew, and a new round begins.

It is important to note that the instructor makes no corrections. A great deal of peer teaching goes on in such an activity. For example, one girl in her excitement and frustration started tearing at her mouth because she could not think of the right word to finish her question. Another student who was thinking along similar lines followed her question and supplied the missing word. The girl's relief was so great that she shouted "yes" in Hebrew. She will never forget that word! This exercise includes the following important activities for the foreign language class:

(1) Seeking information,
(2) Giving information,
(3) Hiding one's intentions,
(4) Problem solving, and
(5) Displaying one's achievements.

GUILTY PARTY

This is basically a problem-solving activity:

(1) A volunteer is chosen who agrees to be the guilty party. This student leaves the room.

(2) The class, in Hebrew, decides on a particular felony this student has committed, and the guilty party is asked to return to face his accusers.

(3) It is the volunteer's responsibility to find out from his accusers what his felony is—without asking, "What did I do wrong?" I gave no assistance on how to go about this; I was interested to see what the students would do on their own. Usually they asked questions of the following type:

(a)   When do I do this? (They did not know past tense yet.)
(b)   Where do I do this?
(c)   For what do I do this?
(d)   Is anyone with me when I do this?

This goes on until the accused makes a guess. If the party cannot arrive at the crime, the class usually tells the student.

(4) The accused is not finished, for he must then defend himself and hope for acquittal. He pleads his case to the class, the class votes, and sentence is passed.

One student was accused of hijacking a plane to Cuba. Having discovered his crime, he asked the class if it were an El-Al airplane. The class responded with an unfriendly, "No!" The defendant then asked if anyone in the class "sees me on the night I take the plane?" A student responded that he had indeed seen him, and that he had a picture of him on the airplane. Defendant: "I want to see it!" (There is a picture of an airplane with passengers on the bulletin board.) The witness walked up to the picture, pointed to a passenger, and exclaimed, "Here you are!" The defendant got up from his chair, took a victory breath, marched over to the picture, and uttered his vindication: "On the plane you can see the name El-Al. You say that the plane I take is not El-Al, and you say that here I am on this El-Al plane. Then I cannot take the other plane to Cuba!" This turn of events angered the class, and they immediately sentenced him to life in Hebrew school.

The Hebrew used was unabashedly atrocious, but everyone was getting the general idea. Particularly crucial mistakes were noted after the round was completed. These errors were items we had covered in drills and explanations, and the comments were very brief. Everyone gets practice in the following with this activity:

(1) Problem solving,
(2) Seeking information,
(3) Giving information, and
(4) Talking one's way out of trouble.

DIRECT LINE TO HEBREW

The intent of this activity was to have the students speak Hebrew on the telephone with a native speaker. A group of cooperative Israelis agreed to help and were appraised in advance of the vocabulary and structures the students should have control of.

(1) Each student is given the phone number of a native speaker.

(2) The student must call, introduce himself, and indicate why he is calling—in Hebrew, of course.

(3) The student must find out a task that has been planned for him and that the native speaker is ready to give to the student. For example, in coordination with the "have to do something" structure students were working with, one task was, "You have to bring a prayer book to Hebrew school tomorrow."

(4) It is the student's problem to arrive at an understanding of the task if he does not immediately grasp what the native speaker is communicating.

(5) The student should thank the native speaker and make a proper farewell.

(6) The student should complete the task assigned and be prepared to give the class in Hebrew a summary of the phone conversation and the resulting activity.

Students were a bit nervous but anxious to give it a try. They were very pleased with how pleasant the native speakers were. The students were told that they were speaking with people that did not know English. However, one student reported that at the end of the conversation the Israeli blurted in perfect English, "You speak Hebrew very well." The student was shocked and quickly hung up. This has created a credibility gap which has to be remedied. Nevertheless, this is an extremely valuable experience. The feedback from the Israelis also proved interesting and beneficial. They could spot immediately those who felt secure with the language regardless of mistakes and those who were stiff and afraid to relax. Those students who were stiff indicated that they saw just how far patterned dialogues and practices would take them, and they wanted to try the telephone conversation again.

Students get practice in the following areas with such activities:

(1) Practice in establishing social relations and polite formulas,
(2) Problem solving,

(3) Giving information,

(4) Seeking information, and

(5) Displaying one's achievements.

RADIO FREE HEBREW

This activity involved the creation of a typical radio program in Hebrew. The following steps involved class and instructor participation in the creation of the program.

(1) The class as a whole decided on the program format.

(2) The decisions regarding program format were reached by the students' listening to a number of radio programs to determine the specific communications in a typical radio broadcast and the order in which these communications occur. This was done outside of class, and students were asked to make lists of the various items they learned from their listening.

(3) Students brought their lists to class, and we put all the various activities on the board. The class then made the choices for their program.

(4) The students decided on the following format:

Announcer:	Sign-on and station identification,
Announcer:	Announces a song to be followed by news,
Song,	
News:	Political-social, sports, interview with prominent personality,

Commercial,
Song,
Weather,
Special bulletin,
Time,
Israeli national anthem,
Sign-off.

(5) Students volunteered for the parts they wanted to help create. Some students were individually responsible for parts; others worked in pairs, for example, in creating the interview with a prominent personality. The creator was also responsible for being the broadcaster for his or her part in the program.

(6) The following limitations and procedures were placed on the students while creating their parts in class:

(a) Vocabulary, for the most part, had to come from what students had already worked with.

(b) No dictionaries were allowed.

(c) Students who did not know how to express an item in Hebrew had to go to other individuals and ask in Hebrew, "Do you know how to say 'x' in Hebrew?" or some other appropriate question.

(d) Only as a last resort could a student go to the instructor. The attempt was to use as much peer teaching as possible.

(e) Once students completed their individual contributions, they made copies of their parts. These copies were then distributed randomly so that no one got his/her own part back. Students were told to correct any errors in vocabulary usage and grammar.

(f) Students underlined what they thought was wrong, and the papers were returned to their authors, who were instructed to look over any errors pointed out by the other students. If a student disagreed as to the presence of an error or if a student did not know how to correct an error, the instructor held short conferences to clear up these items.

(g) Students were told to go home and learn what they wrote, not for purposes of memorization, but for expressive delivery in imitation of radio announcers. Students were told that during the broadcast delivery they could have their notes but should maintain eye contact with the audience.

The remainder of the time before the "broadcast" was spent in rehearsing. The program, which was "broadcast" before 200 people during evening services at the synagogue, was very successful. Those in attendance also received an English script.

This activity proved to be valuable and productive. It is meaningful, spontaneous (even with limitations), and open to the originality and creativity of the students. It also provides a creative outlet for quiet students. For first-year students, the kinds of things they were able to express were an achievement of which they were justly proud. Involved with this project are real interaction activities of:

(1) Entertaining,
(2) Displaying one's achievements,
(3) Giving information,
(4) Learning to make or do something,
(5) Problem solving, and
(6) Establishing social relations.

The activities discussed are exercises in "skill-using" following "skill-getting" activities. Each exercise is an attempt to have students use the target language in typical situations where they are accustomed to using and hearing their native language. They let the student overcome his or her fear of using the language in fairly real situations without the anxiety of immediate negative reinforcement. Enabling the student to muster up the courage to communicate in the language takes place in a non-threatening, freestyle framework where all help each other. Students in Hebrew classes where these activities were introduced showed dramatic and gratifying changes. Their efforts to complete the skill-getting exercises became more intense and successful because they wanted to try their ability with a new structure in a skill-using activity. Communicative-interaction activities, of course, did not end all of the problems in Hebrew school, but their motivating capabilities were very high. At the same time, students began early to grow with their new language, using it and their wits for the real thing—communicating!

NOTES

1. "Talking Off the Tops of Their Heads," in *Speaking in Many Tongues: Essays in Foreign-Language Teaching,* expanded 2d edition. (Rowley, Mass.: Newbury House, 1976), 21-35.

2. "The Sequencing of Structural Pattern Drills," *TESOL Quarterly,* 5 (1971), 197-208.

3. *Language, Psychology and Culture* (Stanford, Calif.: Stanford University Press, 1972).

4. *Op. cit.,* 22.

5. *Ibid.,* 23.

6. *Communicative Competence: An Experiment in Foreign-Language Teaching* (Philadelphia: Center for Curriculum Development, 1972).

7. *Op. cit.,* 29.

8. For a detailed discussion of these classes of drills, see Paulston, *op. cit.*

9. Mary Newton Bruder, *MMC: Drilling for Oral Proficiency in English* (Pittsburgh: University of Pittsburgh, 1972), p. 38.

10. *Ibid.,* p. 38.

11. *Ibid.,* pp. 38-39.

12. Rivers, *op. cit.,* 28.

SKILL-USING, SELF-EXPRESSION
AND COMMUNICATION:
EXERCISES IN THREE DIMENSIONS[1]

Sidney N.J. Zelson
State University College of New York at Buffalo

Portions of this article were previously published by National Textbook Company, Skokie, Illinois.

Most foreign language programs in our schools today, and the textbooks that have been written for them, reflect one single orientation, which dominates the pace, the content, the approach, and, indeed, the attitude of the instructor, directly and indirectly. The language goals of such a curriculum will include, at best, four-skill control of a given body of phonological, grammatical and semantic structures. If classroom activities and materials are any indication, it is thought that the learner who succeeds in reaching such a set of goals will "know" the languages. However, just as the student of mathematics may master any number of processes and manipulations without demonstrating ability to solve story problems that require only a few of such operations, the language student may reach similar mastery of a group of features and lack the ability to recombine them to express himself. He may have achieved *linguistic competence* without having achieved *communicative competence*.

As the language learner attempts to send and receive information in realistic situations, complex cognitive processes come into play. In order to formulate a personal message, he must cope with the following questions:

(1) What linguistic features are there to choose from?

(2) What elements combine with what others?

(3) What rules govern these combinations?

(4) What cues are there to guide me in my choices? [applicable to (1) and (2)]

(5) If there is more than one choice, what is the difference between them that makes one alternative more acceptable than the others?

(6) How can I use, or avoid using, a particular feature or structure that I do not control sufficiently? (Inevitably, the student will acquire varying degrees of control of the linguistic units, sets and systems that are parts of his lessons.)

Still another set of questions must be answered by the learner as he assumes the role of listener or reader:

(1) What are the significant features and units?

(2) How should they be grouped?

(3) What is the message?

(4) Are any parts missing, and if so, how can I figure them out?[2]

Only when he can cope successfully with the processes described above can the student be said to have achieved full communicative competence.

In a construct that is admittedly more intuitive than empirical, *linguistic competence* and *communicative competence* may be considered parts of a larger complex, which would be designated as *proficiency*. There is need for a "proficiency-oriented" curriculum, one that teaches the whole rather than many of its parts. In such a curriculum the student would necessarily start with discrete learning tasks but he would finish with the ability to integrate and actually use what he had learned. In order to achieve this goal of real language proficiency with currently available texts, many of which aim solely for linguistic dexterity, the language teacher will need to create skill-using activities of his own to supplement the skill-getting exercises of the text. The following pages present model activities for such an undertaking.

If classroom language practice is to resemble real language use, students must be presented with problems to solve.[3] As we arrange series of progressively difficult tasks for them to perform, we should keep in mind that each should incorporate as many as possible of the following features:

(1) involves problem solving; e.g., a recombination of various elements,

(2) draws the student's attention and keeps it;

(3) is personally meaningful: the learner will be expressing his own thoughts;

(4) is attainable by everyone in the group (with preparation previous to class, if necessary);

(5) is loosely structured or open-ended;

(6) requires the student to use everyday language;

(7) reinforces text materials;

(8) lies within reasonable boundaries of a real-life context (though teachers and students may often enjoy a whimsical situation);

(9) contains a communicative task, affords practice with a specific language feature or culture feature, or both.

It is worth noting that a great many of these characteristics may be seen in the linguistic activities of one who learns a language outside of the class but rarely in the linguistic activities in the classroom itself.

In the preparation of language tasks, it is useful to think in three dimensions: (1) the theme of the chapter, unit or section; (2) the format of the exercise and (3) the specific structure or grammatical category, or cultural elements, with which we want to practice.

The first dimension might include such possibilities as the following: greetings and introductions, family, meals and foods, friends and acquaintances, vacations, entertainment, music, sports, traveling, shopping, daily living, at the doctor's office, school and studies, time, weather, working, plans for the future, etc.

Another dimension of the exercise is the format itself. Several may be suggested, each with its possibilities of modification. It goes without saying that textbooks on foreign language pedagogy and the teaching of English as a second/foreign language offer additional types.

(1) THE INTERVIEW

Each student is asked to prepare five questions to ask the instructor, who answers them during the next class. After some two or three days of this activity, ten or fifteen minutes at the most each time, two or three students take over the responsibility of answering in the question session. Later on, a different group of students will respond to the questions.

(2) EXPANDED SENTENCES

The instructor, or group leader, gives a sentence to the first participant, who repeats it, adding a thought of his own and using a new element of the same grammatical, semantic, or cultural category. The second participant repeats the sentence of his classmate and adds his own element. The third, the fourth and the fifth do the same in their turn; for example (but in the target language):

a. *I'm not going out tonight because I have to write a letter.*
b. *I'm not going out tonight because I have to write a letter and study for an exam.*
c. *I'm not going out tonight because I have to write a letter, study for an exam, and wash dishes.*

This format may be used in other ways:

a. *My sisters are ugly,* to which other students might add *fat, tall, lazy, stupid,* and other descriptive adjectives that seem appropriate.
b. *I spend Saturdays studying,* to which others might add *writing compositions, sleeping, working, playing the piano, playing football, etc.*
c. *I want to see the Prado,* to which others might add such well known sights of Madrid as *Ciudad Universitaria, Plaza Mayor, Puerta del Sol, etc.*
d. *To prepare gazpacho you need tomatoes,* to which students would add *garlic, cucumber, onion, olive oil,* etc.

(3) TASK ASSIGNMENT[4]

The pupil is instructed to obtain certain items of information from a classmate and to report to his group what he has found out. He receives his directions in English, but for his information-seeking activities, his classmate's responses, and his report only the target language is used.

Example:
Find out where Student X is from, if his family is large, how many brothers and sisters he has, the age of each one, and where they work or attend school.

(4) MONOLOGUE I

Using one structure or grammatical category, the student makes a short commentary, written or spoken, on one or a few aspects of his life. His instructions are given to him in English.

Example:
Tell us five incidents, or things that other people have done this week, that displeased you. Also tell us five things that you have done that may have displeased others.

(5) MONOLOGUE II

In a very limited grammatical and situational context, the student makes a short commentary on a given topic.

Example:
Your parents feel that you should invite a certain classmate, the son of friends of theirs, to spend Saturday at your house. You are not at all interested in furthering your acquaintance with him, but they have brought it up many times. Describe your classmate—his behavior in school, his physical appearance, his personal qualities, etc.—in such a way that your parents will not bring the matter up in the future.

(6) MONOLOGUE III

The student is given a situation and is asked to discuss it at somewhat greater length than in the two preceding exercises. The additional element of creative thinking is introduced to the activity.

Example:
In the state where you live now, a law has been passed that requires people to walk on all fours except when they are indoors or entering or leaving a vehicle. You have returned to your old home town to visit friends. Describe your life now, mentioning the changes that have come about due to the new law.

(7) GAMES

Most language games call for mechanical, low level, or trivial language behaviors. However, the following games require a higher type of performance and/or make the participants communicate with each other:

a. Guess Who? Guess What?

In this game the participants guess at the identity of a character, make up information questions that elicit an already formulated statement that has been furnished to them,[5] or guess what the leader of the group is thinking about. For the first and third types the participants may ask yes-no questions of the group leader or he may give them a series of clues in verbal or pantomime form.

b. Artist

A person looks at a picture and describes it to his teammate, who must try to draw it from his partner's instructions.

c. Birds of a Feather

Each participant has a list of personal data. He looks for all those in the class that have the same as he. He forms his group by asking information questions (questions that use interrogatives).

d. Finish the Sentence

The leader begins a sentence and each participant, in turn, adds a word. The only requirement is that the added word be appropriate in form and meaning. The instructor may structure the exercise, to a certain degree, by his selection of grammatical structure and vocabulary items as he begins. It is useful to outlaw coordinate conjunctions in this exercise.

Examples:
I don't believe that parents of today . . .
It is important that young people . . .
In spite of . . .

e. Hangman

A variation of this well known game calls for the participants to fill in sentences rather than words, as they guess at letters that might properly fill the blanks. A benefit of this game is that students will have practice making inferences from structural and semantic elements and from any other information that they might be able to extract from the various known segments.

(8) VALUES CLARIFICATION

Values and preferences can serve to stimulate interaction in the foreign language. The following techniques focus on the affective domain:

a. The student chooses one activity, place, type of person, or even food, that he prefers, from several alternatives, and comments on why he likes that particular one;
b. The student places himself on a continuum between two opposite words or expressions. He then explains or qualifies his position;
c. The student completes sentences, expressing his own thoughts, values, and opinions;
d. The student draws his "Line of Life" and explains it.

After the members of the group have carried out their tasks and explained, justified or clarified themselves, each one may reiterate a classmate's response and make further comment.[6]

(9) CONTEXTUALIZED PRACTICE IN PAIRS OR SMALL GROUPS

In this example each participant brings an old photograph which serves as a focal point for practicing interrogative structures.

Directions:
Using question words, ask six questions of your partner that will elicit information about the picture. Use at least five different interrogatives. Switch roles with your partner.

(10) ROLE-PLAYING

A situation is presented to a small group of students, who may prepare their parts, if necessary, and act them out. We may avail ourselves of several types, going from a highly structured activity to a less controlled one.

a. Students role-play a familiar conversation pattern, i.e., taking/ giving an order in a restaurant, bargaining with a shopkeeper, making an appointment with a doctor, greeting people formally or informally, formal and informal introductions, etc. A list of useful words and expressions could be furnished to the students and the dialogue could be given to them with several utterances already filled in.[7]
b. The instructor plays the part of a mono-lingual English speaker and two other students take roles of a bilingual and a mono-lingual speaker of the second language. The instructor is able to guide the conversation and, thus, to control somewhat the grammatical and lexical content.[8]

c. Each participant is given a card containing information with which he must operate in the role-playing situation. He is allowed to see his card only.

Example:
Student One, you would like to arrange a three-week tour to England, France or Spain, whichever might be the most reasonable this summer. You need the following information: (1) Which is the cheapest? (2) What is the cost? (3) What does it include? (4) When does it leave? (5) Are guides provided? (6) Would it be cheaper without a guide? (7) What cities will you visit? (8) What points of interest are on the itinerary? (9) Are meals extra? (10) Are there side trips, and how much are they? (11) What is the food like? (You are very particular and don't enjoy food to which you are unaccustomed.)

MAKE NOTATIONS OF ALL INFORMATION THAT YOU OBTAIN.

Student Two, your travel agency has three-week tours to England, Spain and France. The English tour is cheapest at $980, but you get a lot more for your money on the one to Spain, since breakfasts and suppers are included. Groups on this tour will have lodging at three-star hotels. You have heard that the meals and the hotels you use are mediocre, so you should be truthful but as vague as possible about their quality. The tour to Spain costs $1050 for twenty-one days and twenty nights. Groups leave every Saturday from New York. Included in the price are two days in each of the following cities: Seville, Córdoba, Granada, and Segovia. The group will spend a day in Toledo. The remaining time is to be spent in Madrid. There are side trips available to Barcelona for three days and to Mallorca for three days. Each of those costs $100 extra. A very valuable part of the travel package is the service of bilingual guides, who will meet your every need and make your trip all the more enjoyable and educational. Other information will be found in travel folders, which you will have to send, as they will not be available until later this week.

d. The small group is given a short summary of a conflict situation, often a humorous one, with few guidelines. They may be interested in performing them in English first, as it often aids them in their creative efforts, and also gives them an idea of words and expressions for which they will need help from the instructor.

Example:
Your family and another family have gone on vacation together and rented a cottage. As might be expected, your friendship has been subjected to somewhat of a strain after two weeks of togetherness. At last it is over. Complain to and about each other: i.e., eating habits, housework, children, etc.

(11) DISCUSSION AND DEBATE

One may find many useful and interesting topics in such areas as current affairs, value systems, politics, trends in our own country and abroad, topics of personal interest, books, stories, and movies.[9] Advice to the lovelorn columns, such as "Ann Landers" and "Dear Abby" also provide many entertaining and provocative discussions in intermediate or advanced classes.

In creating interaction activities for his students, the teacher would do well to examine them from several standpoints. Language tasks may, for example, be designed to have either two or three dimensions. To construct a two-dimensional activity the teacher begins with a theme or situational topic, in many cases suggested by the text, and then selects a compatible and appropriate exercise format. A third dimension comes into play when the activity is constructed in such a way that the participants will use primarily one or two grammatical structures. Limiting the number of structures to be practiced considerably simplifies the communicative task of the student; yet he is still permitted the satisfaction of being able to participate in an exchange of information. The tasks which follow include examples of both two-dimensional and three-dimensional exercises.

a. **Theme or Situational Topic:**[10] **Daily Life/The Family**
Format: Role-playing

Example:
Complain about all the injustices that you suffer at the hands of your parents, sisters and brothers. Your partner is to make excuses for each offense, defending the other members of your family but, at the same time, not shifting the blame to you. You must insist how terrible they are while your partner maintains their innocence, or minimizes their guilt.

b. **Situational Topic: Foods**
Format: Task Assignment
Grammatical Structure: I/you/he/she likes . . . (One of the problem areas in Spanish)

Example:
Ask a classmate which fruits, vegetables, and meats or fish he likes the best and the least. Tell the rest of your group what you have found out.

c. **Situational Topic: Foods**
Format: Monologue I
Structure: Commands

Example:
Tell me exactly what to do to make a Spanish omelet.

d. **Situational Topic: Daily Living**
Format: Monologue I
Structure: Familiar commands

Example:
Write a letter to your son or daughter who has gone to study at a college in another city. Tell him/her seven things to do and seven things not to do.

e. **Situational Topic: Common Articles**
Format: Games
Structure: The verb(s) *to be,* prepositions

Example:
Try to guess what I am thinking of. Ask me yes-no questions. The object is in plain sight.

f. **Situational Topic: Friends and Acquaintances**
Format: Expanded Sentences
Structure: Subjunctive in relative clauses

Example:
I want to marry somebody who has a rich family.

g. **Situational Topic: Studies and the School**
Format: Values Clarification
Structure: Preterit/Passé Composé

Example:
Draw your Line of Life in school, pointing out the ups and downs and speaking of any good or bad experiences that you are willing to share.

h. Situational Topic: The Home and the Family
Format: Contextualized Practice in Pairs
Structure: Third person direct object pronouns

Example:
You often mislay things around the house and blame other people. In a very demanding tone, ask your partner where various things of yours are. He will tell you that he doesn't know, that he hasn't seen them anywhere. Switch roles with your partner after eight items.

i. Situational Topic: Daily Living
Format: Game
Structure: "At_____o'clock"

Example:
Guess at what time I got up this morning. Each of you will tell me that I got up at a specific time. I will tell you whether or not you are correct.[11]

j. Situational Topic: Getting a Room at a Hotel
Format: Role-playing

Example:
Student One, your family inclues you, your husband/wife, two girls 14 and 10, and a boy 8 years old. You would like a room at this particular hotel for the night, because of its location. You are reluctant to spend much more than eighteen dollars. What you usually do is take a double room for the whole family, have the girls sleep in the second bed and the boy on the floor. You would like the two girls to be separated, as they have been at each other's throats all day in the car. You think it would also be nice to put the children in one room and the adults in another.

Student Two, you are the clerk at a moderately-priced hotel. A family of five would like a double room for the night, but you are a little hesitant because the doubles at this hotel are quite small, especially for five people. You have two single rooms, at 12 dollars each, in which you could put extra beds. You also may have available a two-bedroom suite at 21 dollars, but you won't know for a while, a half hour at the most. Explain the situation to the family, answer their questions, and try not to lose them.

From the activities presented here it can easily be seen that there are many possibilities for real language practice within a given situational topic and that their interaction can be built around, if not strictly limited to, a specific structure or group of structures. This paper presents an effort to pull together for the practicing teacher the necessary ingredients for successful communication tasks, to add a measure of creativity whenever possible, and to outline an approach to the development of an organized body of activities. Through such materials the students may build upon their "drill language" and come to use their skills, in and out of the classroom, for the real purpose of language, communication.

NOTES

1. Many categories of exercises have been taken from their original source, S.N.J. Zelson, "A Relevant Curriculum: Linguistic Competence + Communicative Competence = Proficiency" in R.A. Schulz, ed., *Teaching for Communication in the Foreign Language Classroom,* (Skokie, Ill.: National Textbook Company, 1976), pp. 18-32. In most cases they have been redefined or illustrated with other examples to better suit the purposes of this paper.

2. He must fill in the missing information through a grasp of the redundancy of the language and an awareness of phonological, lexical and grammatical probabilities, a perception of interlinguistic, intra-linguistic and extra-linguistic cues, from the particular message. See Aaron S. Carton, "Inferencing: A Process in Using and Learning Language," in Paul Pimsleur and Terrence Quinn, eds., *The Psychology of Second Language Learning.* (Cambridge: Cambridge University Press, 1971), pp. 50-56. See also Bernard Spolsky, "What Does It Mean to Know a Language, or How Do You Get Someone to Perform His Competence," in John W. Oller and Jack C. Richards, eds., *Focus on the Learner: Pragmatic Perspectives for the Language Teacher* (Rowley: Newbury House, 1973), pp. 164-170.

3. The importance of problem-solving to the learning and using of a second language has been expressed, explicitly or implicitly in numerous sources. See John B. Carroll, *The Study of Language* (Cambridge: Harvard University Press, 1953), p. 188; Frank M. Grittner, *Teaching Foreign Languages* (New York: Harper and Row, 1969), p. 135; Dale L. Lange and Bela Banathy, *A Design for Foreign Language Curriculum* (Lexington: D.C. Heath, 1972), p. 87; William E. Bull *Spanish for Teachers: Applied Linguistics* (New York: Ronald Press, 1965), p. 15; Wilga M. Rivers, *Teaching Foreign Language Skills* (Chicago: University of Chicago Press, 1968), p. 76.

4. Terrence L. Hansen and Ernest J. Wilkins suggest a number of such activities in *Español a lo vivo,* Level One, 3rd edition (Lexington: Xerox College Publishing, 1974).

5. The television game, "Jeopardy," is an example of this type.

6. Caution should be taken that the student is not pressured into revealing thoughts and feelings that he prefers to keep to himself. Neither should the instructor use these activities if he is unwilling to participate himself.

7. Many examples of this treatment may be found in Judith Carl Kettering, *Developing Communicative Competence: Interaction Activities in English as a Second Language* (Pittsburgh: University Center for International Studies, 1975).

8. This treatment is described in more detail in Zelson, "A Relevant Curriculum . . ."

9. A wealth of topics is suggested in George Gianetti, "Variety in the Advanced Spanish Class; Emphasis on Art, Music and Drama," in Frank M. Grittner, editor, *Careers, Communication and Culture in Foreign language Teaching* (Skokie: National Textbook Company, 1974), pp. 106-109.

10. A very useful list of situational topics may be found in Mary Finocchiaro, *English as a Second Language* (New York: Regents Publishing Company, 1974), pp. 162-165.

11. Elizabeth G. Joiner, "Keep Them Guessing," *American Foreign Language Teacher,* IV, 2 (Winter, 1974), pp. 16-18.

TEACHING COMMUNICATION

Adrian Palmer
University of Michigan

From *Language Learning,* vol. 20, no. 1 (1970), pp. 55-68.

A language course has two components, the course content and the presentation of that content.[1] This paper deals with the presentation component. The main thesis is that classroom presentation should be directed from the outset toward the development of communication skills since the ultimate goal of language learning is communication. Although learning requires practice, this practice should be communication practice, not pattern practice. This theme will be developed in considering the following four topics:

I. The nature and form of communication practice drills.
II. The psychological preparation of the student to communicate.
III. The introduction of new content in communication practice.
IV. The relationship of communication practice to text and curriculum.

I. THE NATURE AND FORM OF COMMUNICATION PRACTICE DRILLS

In communication practice (CP) drills, the student finds pleasure in a response that is not only linguistically acceptable, but also conveys information personally relevant to himself and other people. The following two examples illustrate the form such drills might take and the rational basis for their use.

a. Example 1

The most important aspect of a sentence is its meaning, not its form. Sentences can often be incorrect in formal respects but still convey the desired meanings, as in "I told him to opens the window." However, a formally correct sentence used in the wrong situation can lead to real-life problems, as with "I ordered the teacher to go open the window." Thus, sentences illustrating a new pattern should not be practiced without paying particular attention to their meanings. If the teacher discovers that his drills require only mechanical responses, then he should use some other technique to lead the student back into communication and away from pattern practice.

The most powerful technique at the teacher's disposal is his ability to verbally create situations which could be relevant to the student's own life and then to force the student to think about the meaning and consequences of what he would say in such situations. An example will make this clear. Let us say that the teacher wants to practice the following pattern:

I WOULD TELL	HIM	TO	SHUT THE DOOR
	HER		TURN ON THE LIGHT
	THEM		BRING SOME FOOD

He could proceed as follows:

1. Make sure the students understand the sentences, or if necessary, translate a representative sentence into the students' native language.
2. Point out the obvious facts about the structure of the sentence, such as:
   a. WOULD + simple form of verb;
   b. The object form of the pronouns HIM, HER, THEM;
   c. TO + the simple form of the verb.
3. Have the students repeat two or three sentences from the pattern several times to make sure that they are making no gross mistakes such as saying "to shutting the door."

The next step is the most important one for the teacher. He must make his students feel that they are communicating an important idea when they use this pattern. One way to proceed is as follows:

CAST: Teacher
               Student—Paul
               Student—Karen
               Student—Susan

TEACHER: "Karen, if you and Susan came to class at 8 a.m. and it was winter and the room was dark at 8 a.m., what would you tell Susan?"

KAREN: (with any luck at all) "I would tell her to turn on the light."

If Karen has trouble understanding the instructions, the teacher should repeat them, explaining the situation again or translating the original sentence. He must insure that Karen understands what she is replying to. If Karen answers correctly then the teacher turns to Paul:

TEACHER: "And how about you, Paul, if you were with Mary and you wanted to read, what would you do?"

PAUL: "I would tell her to turn on the light."

TEACHER: (in student's native language)[2] "You as a boy would tell a girl to do that for you?"

TEACHER: (continuing in the target language) "Paul, if you came alone, and if I was in the room, what would you do?"

This question is of a type which really forces the student to be imaginative. If he answers mechanically, he might say the following:

PAUL: "I would tell you to turn on the light."

At this point the teacher may react rather violently, accusing Paul of being impolite to a teacher and forcing him to see the implication of using the word *tell* in this pattern when addressing a superior. Or alternatively, the teacher might be more oblique and say:

TEACHER: "Then I would throw you out of class!"

This kind of a statement would make Paul and the other students think about the reason for the teacher's statement and reach the conclusion that they should not tell a superior to do something.

Let us see how communication practice and pattern practice (PP) drills differ. In theory, PP does involve a transfer of attention from form to meaning, but in reality the meanings of sentences grouped as they are in PP drills are not particularly relevant either to each other or to the students. His teacher and fellow students will react only if a student's response is grammatically incorrect. In giving correct responses, there is really no need for the student to consider more than superficial grammatical information. There is little or no sense of satisfaction in a correct response that is only grammatically acceptable but does not convey useful information.

In both communication practice and pattern drills, the student must be aware of the grammatical and semantic restrictions on the substituted lexical items. However in CP, the student would also pass judgment on the social acceptability of his utterance, and decide whether or not his utterance is a logical response to the situation. He would picture himself in a certain situation and consider those factors which influence what he would say outside of the classroom. He would consider his age, sex, and social status. He would worry about whether he is being polite or offensive. He would think about what the repercussions of a certain response would be. The inappropriateness of a student's remark is brought to his attention, as in the response: "I would throw you out of class!"

A further difference between the two types of drills is that while the PP drill can be administered by a machine such as a tape recorder, the CP drill cannot. Since communication drills require flexible and human responses (i.e., not flashing lights), then to administer such drills by machine appears impossible. A live teacher is absolutely necessary, and one is forced to conclude what few people really doubt anyway, that for certain tasks machines cannot replace humans. It follows that if communication drills are deemed sufficiently important, then the teacher should spend his classroom time in doing what he *alone* can do. His self-evaluation should include the following question: Could my role in teaching have been handled equally well by a machine? If the answer is "yes," the teacher can only conclude that he is wasting his talents.

b. Example 2

At a very early point in a language program it is advisable to bring the student's creative abilities into play. One way is as follows: The teacher may require each student to prepare a few questions using vocabulary and grammar patterns in the last lesson that was studied. At the beginning of the course these questions will be very simple and short, and the answers will necessarily be equally brief. A simple dialogue, such as the following, can proceed using just a few key words and patterns. Paul has been asked to make up a question to ask in class:

CAST:	Teacher, Paul, David, John, Mary, Bruce.
PAUL:	"Who is taller, John or Mary?"
TEACHER:	"Who are you asking?"
PAUL:	"I'm asking David."
TEACHER:	"Ask him again."
PAUL:	"David, who is taller, John or Mary?"
TEACHER:	"David, do you understand?"
DAVID:	"Yes, I understand."
TEACHER:	"Then answer the question."
DAVID:	"John is taller than Mary."
TEACHER:	"Mary, is David correct?"
MARY:	"Yes, David is correct."
TEACHER:	(speaking in student's native language) "How would you say what David just said?"
MARY:	"John is taller than Mary."
TEACHER:	(in student's native language) "Would you really say that, would you use your own name like that?" (Teacher translates Mary's inappropriate sentence into her native language.) "Now try again."
MARY:	"David is taller than I."
TEACHER:	"Bruce, what did Mary say?"
BRUCE:	"Mary said David is taller than she."

The key to this CP drill is flexibility and relevance to the classroom situation. Several responses are practiced by asking a single question of different people. Also, the question pattern which Paul wanted to practice is repeated in meaningful contexts.

The teacher will have to explain why what a student is saying is incorrect. When there is no simple grammatical explanation then there is often an equally incorrect way of paraphrasing the student's sentence in his own language. Then the student will understand intuitively why he is wrong, and class time will not be wasted while the teacher gets involved in linguistics, semantics, or general confusion.

A variation on the above drill would be to require students to prepare short stories to be presented orally in class, using vocabulary and grammar patterns from past lessons that the students feel need extra practice. The teacher should encourage cleverness and the imaginative use of language even at the price of failing to achieve grammatical perfection. He should also listen with the goal of determining general weaknesses in intelligibility, to which he could then draw the attention of the entire class. The story can be immediately revised with all the students participating in the revision.

After the story has been revised and repeated by the student and retold by the teacher, then it should be discussed in the target language. In the early stages of instruction the discussion will be limited to simple questions about each sentence. Later on, however, the class can discuss the story in light of each student's own personal ideas: What would you do in that situation? Has such a thing ever happened to you? Could the story have been true? and so on. During the course there should be a conscious effort to transfer the responsibility for asking questions and leading discussions from the teacher to the students so that eventually a student will take over the leadership of the class for each discussion period.[3]

II. THE PSYCHOLOGICAL PREPARATION OF THE STUDENT TO COMMUNICATE

A language teacher should instill in his students a number of skills which are more directly related to the students' psychological attitude toward new languages than their direct knowledge about the language. The importance of teaching these skills becomes obvious when one teaches by communication practice since effective communication requires their constant use.

a. Skill in Criticizing One's Own Performance

To communicate effectively in a second language, one must be skilled in evaluating and criticizing one's own speech. The teacher's role is more than one of providing a model for the student, calling attention to his mistakes, and teaching him how to correct them. A teacher should force the student to listen to himself as he speaks, to be able to recall what he has said, and to be able to pass judgment on his own correctness. The teacher must teach the student to become his own critic.

This goal is best achieved in stages. First, the students should be made to consider what other students are saying as a form of extended listening practice. Then, in evaluating each other, they would become aware of their own potential areas of difficulty, and eventually their own errors.

b. Skill in Understanding New or Unexpected Utterances

Communication implies novelty. If all responses were predictable there would be no communication. Thus a student must be taught to take the proper attitude toward the unknown, both in understanding and production.

If a student hears a sentence which he does not understand he has three options: ignore it, ask what it means, or try and figure out its meaning. For the language learner, the third option is the most difficult to take, the second is easier but ultimately less productive, and the first must be avoided. The following is a technique for making the student take the third option.

When a student says, "I don't understand that sentence," the teacher must first decide whether he can realistically expect the student to understand. If he is not expecting too much, then the teacher must assess the student's past performance in class. If the student is one who frequently gives up on sentences which show even slight deviation from previously discussed patterns, then the teacher should conclude that the student has the wrong psychological approach to the new language. In this case he would be doing the student a disservice by directly explaining what the sentence in question means. The teacher has several options. He may repeat the sentence and say "Think about it," then remain silent. This approach is the "hard line" one and is often necessary with a more stubborn student who has the attitude that language learning is memorizing a set of sentences and using only those sentences. The first few times the student is told to "think about it" he might rebel. However he must not be given the answer. Rather, the teacher should pick out another student who does not completely understand either, but who the teacher knows is willing to guess. The teacher encourages this guessing and helps the student by suggesting different directions in which he might think in order to work out the meaning of the sentence.

For example, if the language being taught is Thai, then the sentence under consideration might be one in which many objects and indirect objects are deleted leaving a string of verbs in a row. The student could be prodded into supplying the missing nouns by thinking about the context of the sentence, thus gradually relating the shortened sentence to a more easily understood complete version using details *which are already known to the student.* The class should be made to realize that meeting the challenge of new sentences in class is essential to developing conversational agility outside.

c. Skill in Expressing Concepts

In communicating, a student will often have ideas which he wishes to express in a second language, but cannot, because he lacks the imagination and initiative to *try*. Many times the teacher will realize that although the student's vocabulary background is sufficient he is afraid to deviate from sentences he has practiced, or words he has memorized. This situation often comes up when word-for-word translational equivalents do not exist between the student's native language and the target language. When a student balks at expressing a new concept, the teacher might simply say: "You already know these words W_1 W_2 W_3, etc. Now think of a way you might put them together to express what you want to say." Then the student can struggle with the problem on his own and benefit from the teacher's evaluation of his efforts. He has been forced to take a big step in language learning, one which he will face repeatedly. He now opens his mind to the possibility of making intelligent guesses about how to express himself. His attitude toward language learning has changed.

As in the case of writing stories, students must learn to be innovative and imaginative in classroom conversation. In the classroom, unlike in a language laboratory, there is the unique opportunity for the student to be told whether his unexpected response was correct or appropriate.

Some students may have difficulty using language creatively. Often, however, the teacher can find something in the personality of the student which can be counted upon to evoke new responses. If the teacher realizes that a student has a particular tendency toward joking, he can "set him up" with a situation in which a simple joke would be a nice alternative to a routine answer. "The battle of the sexes" can often be used to set up situations in which girls or boys can defend their supremacy by an ironic or scornful statement or one which involves a humorous presupposition such as: "when did you stop beating your girlfriend?"

Another communication skill which should be encouraged involves evading questions which one does not want to answer or cannot answer. The student should be encouraged to meet a question by asking another one, or to shift a question from himself to another person. He can also be encouraged to poke fun at the question. All of these techniques make it easier for a student with a limited knowledge of a language to converse in that language without long and awkward pauses which result from "being at a loss for words."

In summary, the teacher has the opportunity to teach the student the art of getting along in conversation. This art requires much more than a knowledge of the language. It requires the proper frame of mind, which is an open-mindedness toward possible responses. It requires that creativity be rewarded when it is attempted even if the attempt is a clumsy one. It is certainly an art which cannot be practiced with a tape recorder. It belongs in the classroom.

III. THE INTRODUCTION OF NEW CONTENT IN COMMUNICATION PRACTICE

An important part of language teaching is the introduction of new vocabulary and grammar material in the classroom. Certain ways of doing this are particularly effective because they take advantage of the teacher's feeling for "the appropriate moment" and his knowledge of the direction the course will take. The principle to be followed is this: certain things will have to be "mastered" in a course, but they should be introduced, as they are needed, in context. "Mastery" can be deferred. The following example illustrating the introduction of a vocabulary item will make this point clear.

If the students have been required to use the new language in situations relevant to their own personal lives, and if they are asked questions which relate to their daily activities, they will quickly need to know how to talk about people other than themselves. Early in a course they might be satisfied to refer to their companions by name and to use words such as *boy,* or *father* in order to talk about shared activities. In one text, for example, the word *friend* is introduced relatively late. In using this text, the word *friend* is needed long before it is formally introduced. The problem at this point is that a teacher may resist departing from the contents of a text for fear that students will feel overwhelmed by additional vocabulary. The proposed solution is to introduce the new word in the proper context, when it is needed. With the word *friend* the context and need are usually apparent. The word should also be introduced in such a way as not to put pressure on the students to remember it. It may be written on the board so the students can find it easily when they need to use it. The students may be told that they do not have to remember the word, and it is being introduced as a "convenience for the moment." The final step is to return to the word repeatedly whenever it seems particularly appropriate, but never to demand that the students produce it from memory. If the teacher has been careful to introduce a word which he knows will eventually appear in a text, he has insured that there will be a reward for the students when they reach it. It will be so familiar, and the students will feel so comfortable with it, that remembering the word will be no problem. New grammar patterns can be introduced in the same way.

The teacher should see to it that new material is tied into old material whenever possible. In vocabulary this can be done by pointing out that a word means the same thing as, or the opposite of, an old word. In grammar teaching it is particularly important that a new pattern be used in contrast to old patterns. For example, let us see how we could approach the question pattern in English, WHO + VERB + OBJECT ("Who kicked the table?"). It should be introduced with a lexicon which makes it easy to figure out the grammatical relationships within the pattern. In the sentence above, people can kick tables, but tables cannot kick people. Once this is established, the teacher could change the vocabulary to make the meaning of the new question open to two interpretations: "Who hit Bill?" Here, Bill is capable of hitting and being hit, so it may not be clear to the student whether Bill is the object or the subject of the verb. After it is evident that the students thoroughly understand the new pattern, they should be asked to recall a sentence like the following: "Whom did Mary hit?" The two patterns can then be practiced by having Mary actually hit Bill, and following this with a set of questions about the action which has just taken place. Thus both question patterns are used contrastively with relevance to a single situation.

It is a mistake, however, to *introduce* a new pattern in contrast to an old one with which it might be confused. Many students then worry more about the potential confusion than about the meaning of the new pattern. The need to compare and integrate new patterns with what has come before can be satisfied *after* the new pattern has acquired some real significance for the students on its own. Thus practice in contrast should follow practice in isolation. The same principle holds true with the introduction of vocabulary. Many students will confuse opposites if they are introduced at the same time. To aid these students in remembering, it is best to introduce and practice one member of a natural pair well before the other member is introduced.

IV. THE RELATIONSHIP OF COMMUNICATION PRACTICE TO THE TEXT AND CURRICULUM

a. Text Considerations

A text can be evaluated from two points of view: usefulness to the student and usefulness to the teacher. The student appreciates a text which will provide him with a clear guide to home study. Many PP texts are satisfactory in this respect since they provide a second, i.e., visual, means of evaluating the correctness of his responses to taped drills. This would require that answers to drills be written in the text. The text is also used as a reference book and should provide an index to the place of introduction of vocabulary in the course. If the language is one which lends itself to a systematic display of grammatical material in the form of paradigms or declensions, then such information can be included. The same can be said of phonology if a special *learning alphabet* is required. Finally, the text should provide some material in the form of stories or dialogues which introduce the language in a natural way and summarize the new material of each lesson for the student. Thus (except for one which resembles a computer program or a formal grammar), there are many texts which are satisfactory from the student's point of view.

For the teacher who is interested in CP teaching, a useful text is one which provides a cumulative account of the vocabulary and grammatical patterns presented. A text with this information relieves the teacher of remembering what has been taught before. Then he can easily integrate old material into new patterns.[4]

A text which is effective for CP should introduce all question patterns quickly. The priority for the introduction of grammatical patterns should be based on their usefulness in establishing quick communication rather than on some notion of their relative linguistic difficulty. Early in the course, vocabulary should be introduced which is relevant to the classroom scene (speak, understand, means, repeat, etc.). Surface irregularities such as morphological variants should be introduced gradually so that the burden of remembering them and using them correctly does not make communication difficult. If these priorities are not adhered to, the teacher will observe either or both of the following consequences:

1. Students will be able to communicate but incorrectly.
2. Students will be able to manipulate words correctly in drills but not use this manipulation to communicate effectively.

In its format a text must strike a balance between two extremes. The first extreme is one of supplying too many classroom drills, and, in doing so, preventing the drills from being spontaneous and relevant to the class. The second extreme is one of supplying too few drills and leaving the inexperienced teacher without enough material to conduct the class. Perhaps the solution lies in providing two separate texts, one for the student which serves as a guide to home study and as a reference text, and another for the teacher, one which suggests drills to help him through the initial lessons, and also provides a set of sample communication practice drills which will train him to take a more active role in teaching.

A mark of a good teacher is his attitude toward the role of a text and the way he uses it. One virtue of a text is that it exerts a stabilizing force on the course, for the students as well as the teacher. However, when the latter feels that the direction of a text departs from that which leads to effective communication, he should feel free to deviate from the text. He should not feel bound to do every drill, or require memorization of every vocabulary item which is included in the text, since he can judge their appropriateness for his particular class better than the author could when he wrote it.

b. The Separation of Vocabulary, Pronunciation, and Grammar Classes

If a course is constructed so that the teacher is restricted to only one aspect of language, such as grammar or pronunciation, then the teacher will be unable to use the full range of techniques at his disposal for stimulating his students. If a teacher is expected to spend an entire class period discussing and drilling phonology, and if he conscientiously does this, he runs a tremendous risk of having the students lose interest and start reacting mechanically. Skill which they acquire in the pronunciation class might have very little carry-over into other classes. This is so because the phonology is not taught as part of a communication system but as an independent sound system.

A student will not learn the significance of developing good pronunciation unless it is stressed outside of the context of a pronunciation drill. If he learns to be aware of phonological mistakes in others' speech at the same time as he is concentrating on other things such as meaning, he will be more conscious of his own pronunciation as it affects understanding. If "being understood" is the main criterion for evaluating the adequacy of one's pronunciation, then pronunciation should be emphasized in the classroom whenever it *interferes* with understanding. The student who associates his own pronunciation habits only with the criticism of a "pronunciation teacher" will completely miss the reason for learning how to pronounce a foreign language adequately—so that he will always be correctly understood.

In relation to an entire language course, pronunciation should be a greater concern in the beginning of the course than later on. Those habits acquired at the start of language study will often be very difficult to change. Thus the teacher should stress pronunciation during the early days of class. But he must also draw attention to, and teach, pronunciation at the same time that he teaches grammar or vocabulary. He will find that doing this is not only necessary but adds variety to his teaching.

Finally, students usually say that given a choice they would rather practice several different skills for short periods of time than practice a single skill for an extended period. If the teacher fails to take advantage of this by not planning each lesson to include a modest amount of new vocabulary, grammar, and phonology, he only shows an insensitivity to the psychology of the student, and his language teaching will suffer as a consequence.

c. The Place for Pattern Practice

Effective communication involves the development of several skills. The preceding discussion has centered about the teacher's contribution to the development of these skills. There is, however, one skill to which the teacher has little to contribute. This is the skill of producing speech quickly and smoothly. If a student cannot do this, his audience will find it tiring to listen to him. Manipulative skills such as the rapid production of acceptable speech are developed through repetition, evaluation, and more repetition. The pattern practice drill is suitable for this sort of practice since it is a way of eliciting large amounts of controlled vocalization with immediate confirmation, wherein the vocalization is evaluated as to its correctness. Pattern practice drills thus find their proper place in a total language course in the student's practice outside of the classroom.

CONCLUSION

Within the total language instruction program, communication practice might be only one of several techniques which the teacher could use. However, the principle of teaching students to communicate should underlie the entire program.

Some might argue that teaching communication as I have proposed would be impossible in a large class, but it can be said that it is possible to do very little language teaching at all in a large class. Others might say that the elimination of PP drills from the classroom will result in a class which is more difficult for the teacher to conduct. They will claim that PP drills are easy to construct and administer; however, ease alone is a poor reason for continuing these drills. The results of teaching a language as a medium of vital communication offset the difficulties of administering such a program.

NOTES

1. I would like to thank the following people for reading this paper and offering many helpful suggestions: John Peterson, Laura Strowe, John Upshur, and Ronald Wardhaugh.

2. The assumption here is that it might be difficult at this stage of instruction to explain the problem using the target language only. The implication of this is that the teacher should know the students' native language and use it whenever a point cannot adequately be made in the target language. This knowledge of the language will also make the teacher aware of its interference in second language learning.

3. A technique for transferring discussion leadership from teacher to student is described in Palmer (1968).

4. For an imaginative description of the nature and function of a corpus, see Fries and Fries (1961), especially Chapters 1 and 2.

REFERENCES

Fries, Charles C., and Agnes C. Fries, 1961. *Foundations for English Teaching.* Tokyo: Kenkyusha Ltd.

Palmer, Adrian. 1968. "A Classroom Technique for Teaching Vocabulary." *TESOL Quarterly* 2.2, 130-133.

CREATING CONTEXTS
FOR LANGUAGE PRACTICE

William R. Slager
University of Utah

From *TESOL Quarterly,* March 1973. Copyright 1973 by the Teachers of English to Speakers of Other Languages. Reprinted by permission of the publisher and William R. Slager.

ON SENTENCE CONNECTEDNESS AND
THE NEED FOR CONTEXT

No doubt Jespersen wasn't the first to say it. I'd like to believe that common sense has always been with us—though we seem to lose it now and then—and that language teachers through the years have allowed themselves to wonder from time to time why the sentences in their textbooks weren't more meaningful and relevant. But Jespersen says it better than anyone I know, simply and directly, and that is why I begin with him. In *How to Teach a Foreign Language,* which was first published in 1904, Jespersen insists that "We ought to learn a language through sensible communications" (p. 11). If communication is to be sensible, it must involve—even from the first day if possible—"a certain ✔ *connection* in the thoughts communicated in the new language" (italics mine). He saw, as most of us have come to see, that random lists of words were next to useless: "One cannot say anything sensible with mere lists of words." But he also saw something that many of us were slower to learn: that language lessons built around random lists of disconnected *sentences* are equally difficult to justify.

Even with the impressive advances in language teaching methodology that have been made in the last three decades, it is not difficult to find lessons that violate this principle of "sentence connectedness." But the situation apparently was even worse in Jespersen's time, especially in textbooks written according to what he calls the "old method." In these books, as Jespersen points out, there is generally as little connection between the sentences "as there would be in a newspaper if the same line were read all the way across from column to column." Jespersen then drives home his point by indulging in a game I'm sure all of us have enjoyed on occasion—the citing of outrageous sets of sentences to be found in language lessons. Here are two examples from nineteenth century books. The first set is from a French reader:

1. My aunt is my mother's friend.
2. My dear friend, you are speaking too rapidly.
3. That is a good book.
4. We are too old.
5. This gentleman is quite sad.
6. The boy has drowned many dogs.

Jespersen's comment on these sentences is worth quoting in full: "When people say that instruction in languages ought to be a kind of mental gymnastics, I do not know if one of the things they have in mind is such sudden and violent leaps from one range of ideas to another."

The second set of sentences, from a German reader, was apparently concocted to teach the innocent student the use of the past perfect:

1. Your book had not been large.
2. Had you been sensible?
3. Your horse had been old.

After looking at such examples, we can begin to appreciate the emotional extravagance in Jespersen's rhetorical question: "Could it really have been that kind of schoolbooks that the Danish writer, Soren Kierkegaard, alluded to when he wrote that language had been given to man, not in order to conceal his thoughts, as Tallyrand asserted, but in order to conceal the fact that he had no thoughts?"

Most of our currently available audio-lingual texts have sentences that are much more reasonable than those cited by Jespersen. But in their emphasis on structure, they often fail to pay sufficient attention to vocabulary and meaning, with the result that many pattern practice drills may contain sentences that are only tenuously connected if at all. If, for example, there is a substitution drill in which the student may substitute any adjective in an adjective slot and any noun in a noun slot, the result may look like this:

1. The symbol is necessary.
2. The teacher is important.
3. The lesson is long.

So much for the problem of sentence disconnectedness. But what about the solution? The most obvious way to avoid a list of random and disconnected sentences, of course, is to create a realistic context or situation to which all of the model sentences are related. This approach is certainly not a new one, for the words *context* and *contextualization* were widely used by teachers and textbook writers in the 60's. In fact, as J.G. Bruton points out in 1969: "Among the vogue words used by ELT specialists that crop up ever more frequently in the reviews of new texts is the expression 'contextualisation,' and it is fashionable in current writing to decry 'uncontextualised' exercises of the type which occur, apparently all too frequently, in textbooks and laboratory drills" (1969:76).

The principle of contextualization, then, is well-established. But in this area, as in many areas of language teaching, there is a great gap between theory and practice. The question, as I see it, is not *whether* we ought to contextualize but rather *how* we ought to go about it. It is one thing to accept the idea that we must have meaningful contexts for our language practice; it is something else, as those who have tried it well know, to come up with the right situation lesson by lesson and book by book. Contextualization is not as easy as it may sound.

The main problem—and about this there is general agreement—is one of match-up. Most of our current texts (at least those that are the most sophisticated and the most widely used) are planned around a carefully selected and sequenced set of grammatical structures. This means, in effect, that we are constantly searching for the right context in which to practice those structures; and the result is that many situations, which at first appear to be very useful in terms of student interest and need, do not always match up with the grammatical structure that is to be learned. To put it another way, there is often a conflict between grammar and situation.

In his article, "The Contextually-Patterned Use of English: An Experiment in Dialogue Writing," David Reibel states this conflict very clearly: "Any foreign language drill or classroom exercise," he says, "necessarily involves two variables: a *grammatical* component and a *contextual* component" (1965:63). If I read Reibel correctly, he seems to be saying that it is almost impossible to achieve a balance between the two:

If the grammatical component is kept constant, as is the case, say, of a pattern drill, it must be at the expense of the contextual component, which must be altered for each new sentence, almost invariably in some random, unpredictable way. If, on the other hand, we could allow the grammatical component of the exercise to vary as needed, we could hold the contextual component constant. (1965:64)

Here and elsewhere (see Reibel and Newmark, "Necessity and Sufficiency in Language Learning") Reibel obviously opts for context. The main part of his article is concerned with writing dialogues in which a number of possible "variants of a single line" have what he calls "contextual equivalence." But the price that he pays is, at least for many of us, impossibly high. In essence, he must argue that a command of syntactical points can be acquired without "any systematic attention to the grammatical form of sentences." In short, with the right kind of contexts, grammar is learned automatically and unconsciously, as one learns the grammar of his first language.

I mention Reibel's approach here only to clarify the issues and emphasize the extreme positions that can be taken. My own view—and that of every practicing textbook writer and classroom teacher I know—is that structural grading from simple to more complex is absolutely essential; and that, while there is an inevitable conflict between grammar and situation, it is possible in most instances to achieve some reasonable accommodation between these two components. An ideal lesson, then, artfully combines grammar and context, structure and situation.[1]

SOME GENERAL ASSUMPTIONS

In this section I will present a list of ten assumptions about contextualization, most of which are widely accepted (if not always followed consistently) by textbook writers. The list is suggestive and tentative, one that no doubt needs modification and expansion. I will also discuss here a possible new approach to contextualization, one that, as far as I know, has not received much attention to date. It is an approach which has been suggested by certain psycholinguistic experiments of John Carroll, one that I will call "condition of elicitation."

Since all the assumptions I list below can be found in one form or another in method books and teacher's guides, I should perhaps preface the list with an apology for stating the obvious. My only excuse is that I have found over the years that many of the ideas (which are, for the most part, matters of common sense) are lost sight of with alarming frequency.

1. The situation should be relevant and immediately useful. Pilots should be talking about airplanes. Mechanics should be talking about engines.

2. The content should reflect the level of sophistication of the student and his knowledge of the world. To put it another way, the content can be quite advanced even though the grammatical structure is fairly simple. Teachers working with native-born students in the U.S. (where ESL, unfortunately, has become inextricably associated with "remedial" work) frequently overlook this matter. I have seen Navajo high school students, who have been using English in school from the first grade, patiently and mindlessly going through "What's this? A book. What are these? Books." when they might equally well have been talking about carburetors. Stevick makes this point very well when he says that "any topic may be treated at any degree of linguistic difficulty" (1971:65).

3. The language should at all times be natural. For example, I can think of no situation in which native speakers answer a set of *yes-no* questions with complete statements:

Do you have a match?
Yes, I have a match.
Do you have any money?
Yes, I have some money.

Complete statements can be practiced in situations where declarative sentences are normal—for example, in narration or description.

4. The sentences should have truth value. You do not gain anything (and you lose a great deal) when you ask the student to practice the same set of statements in the affirmative and the negative:

John went to San Antonio.
→ John didn't go to San Antonio.

Either John went to San Antonio or he didn't. The way out of such situations is easy enough: All you need to do is give a list of things that John did, but his brother didn't do. The negative sentences can be practiced with *John's brother.*

5. For beginning students especially, the sentences should be what Stevick has called "light" (1971:47). Lightness, as he uses the term, refers to "sheer physical characteristics." And he recommends that the writer can test for lightness by asking this question: "Does an individual line weigh heavily on the student's tongue, either because of the number of difficult sounds or because of its sheer length?" Too many words or structures can also, of course, contribute to the heaviness of a lesson.

6. If characters are used, they should be readily identifiable, and their characteristics and abilities should be easy to remember. One example here should clarify what I mean. In the original edition of Book Two of *English for Today,* there is a lesson on modal auxiliary *can.* The situation for language practice seems simple enough. We chose five people who could speak both English and Spanish, and five who could speak only English. Then the practice proceeded as follows:

Can (Mike) speak Spanish? Yes, (he) can.
Can (Karen) speak Spanish? No, (she) can't.

The resulting drills, as teachers soon reported, created chaos in the classroom. Since we had chosen ten Anglo characters and had given them no personality whatsoever, the students simply couldn't remember (and couldn't care less) who spoke Spanish and who didn't. In revision, the situation was easily modified. (The suggestion came from Dr. Lois McIntosh of the University of California at Los Angeles, who has taught me a great deal about contextualization.) The revised lesson introduces a Navajo (who can speak Navajo and English), a Mexican (who can speak only Spanish), a Canadian (who can speak French and English), and a Japanese airline hostess (who can speak five languages). Now, hopefully, the students will have little difficulty asking and answering questions with *can*:

Can John Begay speak Navajo? Yes, he can.
Can Pedro Campos speak Japanese? No, he can't.
Can Marie Martin speak Navajo? No, she can't.

7. There should be a variety of "language samples" through which the context is presented. While consistency in format is admirable, the fact is that some structures occur more naturally and frequently in conversation (*Me, too. I don't, do you?*) whereas others occur in exposition, narration, and description. (*After a long discussion, it was determined that many of the old buildings, which were beyond repair, should be torn down to make way for new construction.*) Some textbook writers appear to assume that any language structure can be conveniently presented in dialogue form. This simply is not the case.

8. In setting up dialogues, the social dimension should always be kept in mind—that is, who is speaking to whom and the social status of each speaker. Otherwise there will be no possibility of learning the important distinctions between formal and informal speech. For example:

(Teacher to student)
T: Good morning.
S: Good morning.

T: How are you today?
S: Fine, thank you.
(Student to student. The students know each other well.)
S_1:   Hi.
S_2:   Hi.
S_1:   How're you doing?
S_2:   Pretty good. How about you?
S_1:   Not bad.

The social dimension should also be kept in mind in determining when and to whom one can safely ask such questions as "How old are you?" and "How much money do you make?"

9. The language sample should be short enough so that the student has little difficulty in remembering it, but long enough to provide sufficient practice on the new structure. It is not always easy to decide about length, for there can never be an exact definition of what is too long and what is too short. Let's take an extreme example of both. The dialogues in *Modern Spanish,* Second Edition, frequently contain ten or more exchanges. Many students find memorizing dialogues this long difficult and boring, and they lose interest in the rest of the lesson. On the other hand, a dialogue that has only one exchange will not have in it enough material for drills and exercises. One technique for avoiding excessively long dialogues and prose passages is to break down the dialogue or reading into smaller, self-contained units which can be used as the basis for one or two drills. In this way the students can concentrate on the new language items and they are not needlessly slowed up or confused because they cannot remember the details (the vocabulary or the situation) introduced in the language sample.

10. In devising contexts, care should be given to including sentences that can be used for vocabulary development and communication activities—sentences that can be used as the basis for what Stevick calls a "Cummings device" (1971:59). For example, the following question and answer might occur in a dialogue:

S_1:   Where did you go last night?
S_2:   To a movie.

This question can readily be used to expand vocabulary and encourage realistic conversation by providing the following alternate answers:

Where did you go last night?
To a movie, a game, a concert.
I didn't go anywhere. I stayed home.

Amazingly enough, many of us have ignored the need for alternate responses in realistic language practice. If a student is asked to give a real answer to a question such as "Where did you go last night?" he ought to have the option of answering that he didn't go anywhere.

Let me conclude this section with a brief discussion of a promising new direction which might be taken in contextualization, a direction which, as far as I know, has received very little attention in the textbooks currently available. Simply stated, it takes into account what John Carroll has called the "conditions of elicitation" (1958). That is, it is concerned with the circumstances or conditions under which a speaker will produce a certain kind of sentence.

The need to consider "condition of elicitation" was forcefully brought home to me by a story I heard several weeks ago. Very early in most ESL texts, the students are required to practice the identification pattern. "This is a book." Yet few of us have wondered just when and how often we actually use such a statement. Recently, it seems, an experienced ESL teacher found himself using this sentence and was so amazed that he immediately made note of it. The teacher had gone to the post office in order to mail a book which was carefully wrapped in brown paper. When he went to the window, he said to the clerk: "This is a book." When he recovered from the shock, he began to ask himself why he had said it. The reason is clear enough: As Carroll has postulated, "declarative sentences are normally uttered when the speaker perceives his own information as greater than that of his hearers." Since the man behind the counter did not know what was in the package, he had to be told. The story has an obvious moral: Should we ask our students to "make statements" in order to practice their form, or should we ask them to make statements in a context where a statement is naturally called for?

What I am suggesting is that the ideal context might well go beyond the situation itself to specify the conditions under which the sentences in the language sample are to be practiced. Granted, such precise specification would be difficult, and it might not be possible to achieve in every lesson. Still, the approach is worth trying. It certainly seems more reasonable to ask a question in order to practice question form.

SOME SPECIFIC EXAMPLES

In this section of the paper I will discuss two grammatical structures—the passive construction and the present perfect construction—and the problems involved in creating useful contexts through which they might be practiced. The intent is to provide some insight into the kinds of questions a practicing textbook writer considers in trying to develop sensible and useful situations on which classroom drills and exercises can be based. I hold no brief for the contexts themselves. To resort to the current jargon, it is the process and not the product I am concerned with. Unfortunately, there will be little time to deal with the ways in which these situations might be practiced—with the kinds of drills and exercises, both oral and written, that might be used more effectively.

CONTEXT ONE: ON PRACTICING THE PASSIVE

My first example of contextualization deals with the passive construction. In order to set up realistic situations for practice, the following points must all be considered:

1. In many cases, passive sentences are not merely stylistic alternatives to active ones. With indefinite pronouns, for instance, passive sentences may have a meaning quite different from that of the "related" active form:

Everybody loves somebody/
Somebody is loved by everybody.

Given the assumption that a surface subject receives more emphasis, the question of "focus of attention" becomes important, too. Thus *my neighbor's dog* presumably receives more emphasis in the first sentence below than in the second one:

My neighbor's dog bit me.
I was bitten by my neighbor's dog.

Moreover, when the passive is used because the agent is unknown or of no interest, little is to be gained by "restoring" the subject by means of a "pro=form" such as *somebody* or *someone*:

That house was built thirty years ago.
Somebody (or someone) built that house thirty years ago.

Another critical question with regard to passive sentences is the agent phrase with *by*. In an article on "The Agent in the Passive Construction," L. Mihailovic classifies verbs in four different groups according to whether or not the *by* phrase is obligatory or optional. While the classification is open to question, Professor Mihailovic admirably succeeds in demonstrating the complexity of usage. With verbs such as *break,* for example, the *by* phrase is deletable:

Somebody broke my window.
→ My window was broken.

But with words such as *bring up,* the *by* phrase cannot be deleted unless some kind of adverbial is present:

His uncle and aunt brought him up.
He was brought up in London.
But: *He was brought up.

In view of the complexity of the passive, which I have only been able to touch upon here,[2] it is understandable that many language teachers have become increasingly more suspicious of the limited usefulness of exercises that ask the student to transform a list of active sentences into passive ones. The case against "conversion" exercises is convincingly argued in an article by D. Byrne on "Teaching the Passive" that appeared in *English Language Teaching* several years ago. Such exercises concentrate exclusively on *form,* which is often difficult for the student to master. I should also point out that Carroll's concern with "condition of elicitation" is perfectly applicable here: we simply do not go around making passive sentences because someone has told us to form them from active ones.

2. Several times during the course of a recent revision of the *English for Today* series, Lois McIntosh and I discussed at some length the kinds of contexts through which the passive could be presented. The format that we had frequently followed was one in which a new construction was introduced through a brief dialogue. But when we tried to write dialogues to illustrate the passive, we found that they were often awkward and forced, and we finally concluded that the passive occurs much oftener in description, narration, and exposition than in conversation. This situation may well be what Byrne had in mind when he wrote that "The passive is perhaps most effectively practiced through written exercises . . ." (Byrne, p. 128).

After any number of false starts, we finally came up with some of the following contexts. In planning our lessons, of course, we were obliged to keep in mind the sequencing of tense and verb constructions as well as the occurrence of the *by* phrases.

Situation One: Present Tense
Since the agent is of no consequence, the *by* phrase is omitted.

German is spoken in Switzerland. French and Italian are also spoken there. English is spoken in Canada. In some parts of the country, French is spoken, too. Both English and French are official languages in Canada.

These sentences can be practiced without reference to active sentences artificially constructed with such subjects as *people, they,* or *one*:

People speak French in Switzerland.
They speak French in Switzerland.
One speaks French in Switzerland.

Situation Two: Present Tense

Here the agent is obligatory. Note that "Some people are bothered" would strike a native speaker as somehow incomplete.

Some people are bothered by smoke. Others are bothered by noise. Some people are bothered by crowds. Others are bothered by heavy traffic. Etc.

Situation Three: Simple Past Tense

Here the agent is omitted because it is unknown or is of no importance to the conversation. (A guide is talking about the United Nations building in New York.)

Construction of these buildings was begun in 1950. The Secretariat was completed in 1951. The other buildings were completed in 1952. Etc.

Situation Four: Modal Passive

(Here the guide is talking about city planning and the needs of the city.)

New hospitals must be built. More parking spaces must be provided. The airport must be expanded. Etc.

With the modal passive, we developed a situation in which active and passive forms could be practiced together in what appears to be a natural, uncontrived way:

We have to build a new hospital.
A new hospital must be built right away.

We have to provide more parking space.
More parking space must be provided immediately.

We have to expand the airport.
The airport must be expanded as soon as possible.

Apparently this naturalness is achieved by adding the adverbial, so that the result is a restatement with a different empahsis or focus. Another condition that makes for naturalness is the fact that the "we" of the active sentences is a kind of generalized pronoun and is probably not thought of as an agent. Notice the unacceptability of adding a *by* phrase on the assumption that the passive formula can optionally include an agent:

A new hospital must be built by us.

A new hospital must be built by us right away.

Situation Five: Perfect Passive

The situation is introduced in the form of reading that was adapted from an article in a New York City newspaper. The *by* phrase has no place here. For one thing, the agent is probably not "restorable": There are no doubt a number of "agents" involved—construction companies, contractors, etc. For another, the focus is on what happened to the objects—to the houses, the buildings, the schools, etc.

> An old section of the city has recently been restored. Many changes have been made. Many of the old houses have been repaired. New businesses have been started. One old building has been converted into a theater, and many cultural activities have been developed. Education has not been neglected. New elementary and secondary schools have been built, and a new college has recently been opened. Now this old section of the city is no longer a slum. It has been changed into an exciting place to work and live.

All of the above contexts, as far as I am able to determine, accurately demonstrate appropriate uses of the passive construction. But while a great deal of time was given to the contexts themselves during revision, insufficient attention was paid to the situations in which they should be practiced. If I were to do it again, I would revise some of the drills to take into account Carroll's "conditions of elicitation." In one of his experiments, Carroll provides a useful clue as to one way in which the passive might be elicited. In this experiment, the students watched a professor as he performed various actions with colored blocks. If the students were told to "describe what happened," they overwhelmingly answered in the active: "Professor Smith X'd the blocks." But if the students were told to "Describe what happened to the blocks," the majority shifted to the passive: "The blocks were X'd." Carroll's approach, of course, can only be applied to situations in which the agent is known and a sensible and realistic choice can be made between active and passive.

CONTEXT TWO: ON PRACTICING THE PRESENT PERFECT

This set of examples is concerned with an especially difficult and troublesome construction for the nonnative speaker of English, the present perfect, as in "I've already seen that movie." In discussing the present perfect, W.S. Allen observes that it is "probably the commonest tense in English, but it is one which the student of English usually finds the most difficult to learn" (1959:83). Here, as is often the case, the students have little difficulty learning the form, though they must spend some time memorizing the irregular past participles. The difficulty lies in learning to use the construction in the same situations as a native speaker would.

1. In devising contexts for the present perfect, the need for grammatical insights into its meaning and use is especially crucial. Native speakers, who use the construction in very complex and subtle ways, have no idea of the conditions under which they would choose a present perfect form, say, over a simple past. Consider, for example, how you could account for a choice between these two sentences:

I studied Spanish.
I've studied Spanish.

Either would be equally "grammatical." And your choice would not be governed by when the event actually took place: You could have studied Spanish last month or years ago. The most important condition for selection appears to be how the speaker regards the event in relation to the current situation—in Allen's words, "its effect on events NOW." If, for example, you are simply commenting about the fact that you studied Spanish, you would probably choose the simple past:

S_1:   Do you speak Spanish?
S_2:   No. I studied it when I was in high school, but I can't remember more than a few words.

If, on the other hand, you wish to emphasize that your studying of Spanish is relevant to the current situation, you would probably use the present perfect:

S_1:   Can you translate this article for me? It's in Spanish.
S_2:   Of course I can. I've studied a lot of Spanish.

Twaddell has neatly captured at least part of the "meaning" of the present perfect by stating that it signals "current relevance"—that it "explicitly links an earlier event or state with the current situations" (1965:8-9). If Twaddell is right, then it must be the speaker's view of the situation that governs his choice of present perfect or past.

In an interesting article in *Language Learning*, Robin Lakoff refers to the choice between present perfect and past to illustrate the importance of introducing "contextual factors outside the scope of rules"

(1969:123). There are simple grammatical rules, for example, that will explain why the first sentence that follows is grammatical while the second one isn't:

The book is yellow.
*The books is yellow.

But the choice between the two sentences below, which Lakoff quotes from Jespersen, involves two sentences that are completely grammatical:

The patient has gradually grown weaker.
The patient gradually grew weaker.

The choice is determined by the speaker's knowledge of the situation. In the first sentence, the assumption is that the patient is still alive, while in the second sentence no such assumption can be made. As Lakoff describes it, the nonnative speaker who uses the perfect instead of the past, or the past instead of the perfect, does not sound "ungrammatical." Rather, he creates a "certain confusion" in the mind of the native speaker who is listening to him—a feeling that he is "not using the language right, or does not know something that everyone else in the world knows, or something that he has already said he knows" (1969:124).

This confusion that a native speaker can experience is aptly illustrated by a story I heard just recently from an instructor at Lackland Air Force Base. All of his students were aware of the fact that the instructor had spent some time teaching English in Viet Nam. Thus when one of his students asked him, "How long have you been in Viet Nam?" the instructor was momentarily puzzled. He knew, and he knew his student knew, that he was now in San Antonio. While the student's question was completely grammatical, it was inappropriate, for behind it was the presupposition (one which the student was not aware of) that the instructor was still in Viet Nam. Doubtless experienced ESL instructors everywhere could cite many similar examples.

With the present perfect, then, the careful planning of context is absolutely essential. Many attempts, even by such knowledgeable writers as W.S. Allen, are often notably unsuccessful. Note, for example, Allen's first exercise on the present perfect:

Drill. Books shut.
1. John, open your book at page 3. What have you done? (Allen, p. 83)

Presumably the student is to answer "I have opened my book at page 3." I'm not at all sure how the teacher is to react if the student answers "I opened my book." or "What do you mean? Did I do something wrong?"

2. Now to the contexts themselves. The dialogue form appears to be admirably suited to the present perfect, since conversational exchanges frequently contain that construction. The dialogue is also useful because it allows for the practice of shortened responses using auxiliary *have* where the past participle is understood.

Situation One

The past participle is limited to *been,* and the time expressions emphasized are *ever* and *never*:

S_1: Have you ever been to Europe?

S_2: No, I haven't. Have you?

S_1: I've never been there, but my mother has. She was born in Norway, and she's been back there several times. She's been to France and Germany, too.

Situation Two

Here the time expressions *already* and *yet* are introduced. Jane and Roger, who have recently become engaged, would like to go to a movie alone. Sam is Jane's little brother; Ann is her little sister.

Jane: Roger and I would like to go to a movie tonight. Have you seen any good ones lately?

Sam: I saw "The Lost Explorer" last night. It's great.

Jane: Oh yes. I've heard about the movie, but I haven't seen it yet.

Ann: Well, everyone else in the family already has. I went this afternoon with Kim. And Dad and Mother went last week. I guess you and Roger will have to go by yourselves.

Jane: Yes, I guess we will.

Notice that the present perfect occurs along with the past:

present perfect: *Have* you *seen* any good ones lately?

past: I *saw* "The Lost Explorer" last night.

present perfect: I *haven't* seen it yet. Everyone else in the family *has.*

past: I *went* this afternoon with Kim.

This mixture of forms accurately reflects real speech, for it is often difficult to find a conversation that is confined to a single tense or verb construction.

Situation Three

Here the time expressions *since* and *for* are introduced. Also introduced, for recognition only, is the present perfect progressive. A landlady is talking to three foreign students who have just rented an apartment from her.

Landlady: Have you boys ever been to New York before?

S_1: No, we haven't.

Landlady: How long have you been here?

S_2: Since last Friday.

Landlady: You speak English very well. How long have you been studying it?

S_3: For years. English is a required subject in our country.

Situation Four

This introduces the present perfect progressive. Jane and Roger, now on their honeymoon, are taking a cruise down the Rhine.

Roger: Oh, there you are. I've been looking for you. What have you been doing?

Jane: Unpacking. I've been trying to find a clean shirt for you. I just came up here a few minutes ago.

Roger: You missed some great scenery. We'll be passing the Lorelei Rock any minute.

Jane: I can't wait to see it. They say a beautiful siren has been sitting there for hundreds of years. She's been singing to the sailors.

Roger: Yes. They say men can't resist her.

Jane: I'm going to hold on to you when we pass her rock.

Roger: Don't worry. She's too old for me.

Difficult as it is for the student to learn, the present perfect at least has one attraction for the textbook writer: It is relatively easy to write contexts for. I suspect that at least part of the difficulty that the student has in learning to use this construction is that he is often given only one context in which to practice it and he has little opportunity to contrast it with the simple past tense.

THE TEACHER AS ADAPTER

Throughout this paper the emphasis has been on the role of the textbook writer, on his responsibility for embedding new grammatical structures in contexts that accurately reflect their use. A textbook, then, is properly regarded as a series of lessons, each one of which may be more or less successful in blending grammar and context. Rightfully used, it should be no more than a kind of outline. If this view is accepted, it implies an important creative role for the classroom teacher; for it is the teacher who is ultimately responsible for adapting each lesson to meet the specific needs and interests of his students. The teacher, as well as the textbook writer, must be a contextualizer.

All of which brings us to the subject for another paper, I suppose, a how-to-do-it essay with the possible title of "Teachers and Contexts." At the moment I'm not at all sure just what the ten or twenty easy steps would look like, but I am sure of one thing: The essay would urge the teacher to develop his awareness of language in use, to listen when people are talking and make note of the occasions on which they employ constructions that he has taught or is going to teach. It would urge him, in short, to become a collector of contexts.

The textbook writer has a responsibility here as well. If the teacher is expected to adapt, the writer should do all he can to set up his lessons so that they are readily adaptable. One way in which he can help with adaptation is by making his lessons as "transparent" as possible. The term *transparent* is Stevick's, and he is the one who has suggested that the following question might be used in testing a lesson for transparency:

> How easily can a teacher or adapter find places where he can make changes or additions without destroying the lesson? (1971:48)

Changes and additions will be easier to effect if each lesson is accompanied by a fairly complete set of grammatical notes which identify the language items that are to be taught.

If the teacher clearly understands the grammatical points that are to be emphasized, and if he is given accurate and full explanations of how and when those grammatical structures are used by native speakers of English, he is no longer bound to the text. He is free to create his own situations for language practice, situations which should in most cases be infinitely more effective than those in the book, for they will have content that is interesting, meaningful, and immediately useful to his own students.

NOTES

1. Since writing this I turned up an article by Leslie A. Hill entitled "The Reconciliation of Grading with Contextualization." As the title suggests, his approach is the same as mine.

2. To date, as far as I know, transformational grammarians have not been able to come up with useful generalizations about the passive. Note Robin Lakoff's remarks on this point: "Passivization is a rather touchy subject now among most transformational grammarians who are aware of recent thought in the field. It is embarrassing because, until a few years ago, it was one of the best-understood rules in the grammar." (Lakoff, 1969:130)

REFERENCES

Allen, W. Stannard. 1959. *Living English Structure,* 4th ed. Longmans.

Bruton, J.G. 1969. "Contextualisation," *English Language Teaching* XXIV, 1.76-79.

Byrne, D. 1966. "Teaching the Passive." *English Language Teaching* XX, 2.127-30.

Carroll, John B. 1971. "Current Issues in Psycholinguistics and Second Language Teaching," *TESOL Quarterly* 5, 2.101-114.

———. 1958. "Process and Content in Psycholinguistics," in R.A. Patton (ed.) *Current Trends in the Description and Analysis of Behavior.* University of Pittsburgh Press.

Cole, N.R. 1969. "The Structured Dialogue: An Attempt to Integrate Structural and Situational Approaches to Language Teaching," *IRAL* VII, 2.125-132.

Hill, Leslie A. 1970. "The Reconciliation of Grading with Contextualization," *RELC Journal,* June, 1970.

Jespersen, Otto. *How to Teach a Foreign Language.* George Allen and Unwin, first published in 1904.

Lakoff, Robin. 1969. "Transformational Grammar and Language Teaching," *Language Learning* XIX, 1 & 2.117-140.

Mihailovic, Ljiljana. 1966. "The Agent in the Passive Construction," *English Language Teaching,* XX, 2.123-126.

Newmark, Leonard and David A. Reibel. 1968. "Necessity and Sufficiency in Language Learning," *IRAL* VI, 2.145-164.

Oller, J.W. and D.H. Obrecht. 1968. "Pattern Drill and Communication Activity: A Psycholinguistic Experiment," *IRAL,* 6.165-174.

———. 1969. "The Psycholinguistic Principle of Informational Sequence: An Experiment in Second Language Learning," *IRAL* VII, 2.117-124.

Reibel, David A. 1965. "The Contextually-Patterned Use of English: An Experiment in Dialogue Writing," *English Language Teaching* XIX, 2.62-71.

Rivers, Wilga M. 1968. *Teaching Foreign Language Skills.* University of Chicago Press.

Sager, J.C. 1969. "Language Laboratory and Contextual Teaching Methods," *IRAL* VII, 3.217-231.

Stevick, Earl W. 1971. *Adapting and Writing Language Lessons.* Foreign Service Institute.

Twaddell, W.F. 1965. *The English Verb Auxiliaries,* 2nd ed. revised. Brown University Press.

(**8**)

DEVELOPING AND EVALUATING
COMMUNICATION SKILLS
IN THE CLASSROOM

Rebecca M. Valette
Boston College

From *TESOL Quarterly,* March 1973. Copyright 1973 by the Teachers of English to Speakers of Other Languages. Reprinted by permission of the publisher and Rebecca M. Valette.

In his introduction to the Lackland lectures of 1972 (as they appear in the March, 1973, issue of the *TESOL Quarterly*), Maurice Imhoof stresses that "all [papers] concern themselves with the creation of a classroom environment in which genuine communication takes place."[1] The two key elements of this statement, namely "classroom environment" and "genuine communication" seem contradictory at first glance. The foreign language classrom is by its nature an artificial environment in which traditionally only artificial communication has taken place. Genuine communication in a foreign language, on the other hand, has generally occurred outside the classroom, and most frequently in the country where the language is spoken. In the language classroom, the evaluation techniques were developed to test the student's control of structure, vocabulary and phonology, and at best to measure his proficiency in artificial communication situations. In the real out-of-the-room environment, where the student was engaged in genuine communication, he himself was usually the only one evaluating his ability to understand and to express himself in the new languages. "Yes, I can understand that sportscaster." Or "No, I only get about half of what he is saying." Often we hear adults say: "I had three years of Spanish in school but never learned to speak it." What they are saying is that although they received respectable grades for their classroom performances, these grades, at best, reflected artificial communication activities. Genuine communication was either totally lacking in the curriculum or so lightly touched on as to seem nonexistent in retrospect. In any case it was probably not at all tested.

This brings us to a key aspect of the classroom environment, namely formal evaluation. In the classroom this evaluation is carried out directly by the teacher or indirectly by some measuring device ranging from the formal standardized test to the built-in steps of a programmed course. The nature of this evaluation, that is, the content of the tests and the method in which grades are assigned, reflects more accurately than any lengthy statement of aims and purposes, the real objectives of instruction. The way in which the tests are adminstered, the manner in which test results are used and interpreted, and the basis on which grades or evaluations are prepared, in short, the evaluation technique, sets the tone for the foreign language class. In this paper I should like to suggest some means for developing and evaluating the communication skills in the classroom.

All of us know what is meant by communication in a foreign language, namely, the ability to understand what one hears or reads, and the ability to express oneself in speaking and writing. The problem over the centuries has been *how* to inculcate in students this ability to communicate in a second language, given the constraints of a classroom environment and, most often, a classroom which was not located in the country where the language was spoken. The big fallacy has been the conviction of many language teachers that the student by mastering the elements of language (patterns, words, phonemes) would eventually acquire skill in communication. Some students did indeed make the jump, either because they were "natural" learners, or because they had the opportunity to visit or reside in the country where the language was used. Most did not.

Let me draw a quick analogy between language learning and the act of skiing. We were in the French Alps last year, within easy driving distance of the ski resorts. Thanks to much reading, I could easily explain how to do various turns and could pick out those skiers who did them well. It was quite another thing when I myself was coming down the slope. My natural reflexes were not those of a skier and in the tricky situations, for example when I was accelerating faster than I wanted to, I would do all the wrong things, even though in my mind I could have explained what all the right things were. When faced with a free conversation or a free composition, our language students are frequently in the same position that I found myself in on the slope. They are accelerating, that is they know what they want to say or write and are in a hurry to express themselves, and they come out with constructions that reflect their native language, rather than the language they are trying to use. These students are usually able afterwards to point out many of their mistakes. What they need is not remedial grammar review but rather additional opportunities for free expression, just as my skiing would improve if I spent more time on the slopes. Of course, there are times when the students cannot remedy the errors without the help of the teacher, just as the novice skier benefits from the advice of the instructor. But on the whole, one learns to communicate in a foreign language by communicating, to state the obvious fact.

The nature of second language learning has long intrigued the theoreticians. Simon Belasco, for example, divides the language learning process into three stages: pre-nucleation, post-nucleation and mastery.[2] In the first phase, that of pre-nucleation, the student acquires elements of language: the sound structure, the syntactic structure and the sandhi variations. When the student can systematize these elements, that is, when he can create and understand sentences built of these elements, he has reached the stage of nucleation. In the post-nucleation stage he gradually develops the communication skills, hopefully arriving at the level of language mastery.

Wilga Rivers, in her 1971 Lackland lecture, presented a model of the essential processes in language teaching which contains two major stages: skill-getting (subdivided into cognition and production or pseudo-communication) and skill-using.[3] The cognition refers to the knowledge of units, categories and functions in the areas of phonology, structure and lexicon, whereas the production or pseudo-communication stage refers to the student manipulation of the language via learning sequences such as drills, exercises and other guided activities. At the level of skill-using the student is motivated to communicate, that is, he is acting as an autonomous individual interacting with other individuals.

In several of my writings, I have been developing a taxonomy of language learning objectives adapted from the Bloom taxonomies.[4] The first three stages are Mechanical Skills, Knowledge, and Transfer. Mechanical Skills refer to phonology and spelling. Knowledge subsumes the learning of vocabulary, sentence patterns, grammatical rules. Transfer is the stage at which the student manipulates these "bits and pieces" of language in new ways, under the guidance of the teacher of the learning materials. The fourth stage is Communication in which the student actually uses the language to express himself and to understand things said and written in that language.

If you compare these three models, you will notice that Belasco's pre-nucleation phase may be equated with Rivers' skill-getting activities and with my first three taxonomical stages: Mechanical Skills, Knowledge and Transfer. And just as Belasco points out the need of developing courses at the post-nucleation level which stress audio-comprehension and reading which in turn lead towards proficiency in speaking and writing,[5] so Rivers in her second Lackland lecture stresses classroom activities which would lead the students from pseudo-communication to communicative competence.[6] I, too, in my book, *Modern Language Performance Objectives and Individualization,* insist that teachers set communication goals for their classes, rather than focusing uniquely on goals in the Taxonomic stages of Mechanical Skills, Knowledge and Transfer. (See Figure 1.)

You may wonder why, if such unanimity of purpose exists among certain foreign language theoreticians, a problem exists. Most teachers, if asked whether they were teaching vocabulary, pronunciation, grammar or communication skills, would invariably answer that they were teaching communication. But are they?

One problem here is that of semantics: the expression "communication skills" has lost its original meaning. This occurrence can be traced back to the 1960s when the proponents of the audio-lingual approach stressed the need for teaching four skills: listening, speaking, reading and writing. They were, I believe, correct in their emphasis. But what happened was that teachers began to equate the perception of phonemic differences with listening, the recitation of dialogs with speaking, the deciphering of printed characters and the mastery of sound-symbol correspondences with reading, and prepared dictations and written drills with writing. In other words, skill-getting techniques were confused with the ability to use skills. The *mode* by which the elements of language were mastered—receptively through hearing and seeing the printed word; productively through vocalizing and copying or putting these elements on paper—was not distinguished from communicative competence or the ability to use the foreign language for interaction.

As I mentioned earlier, the best way of verifying what goes on in a classroom is to look at the testing system used by the teachers. The purpose of the taxonomy of objectives which I briefly sketched for you

Figure 1.   Three Models of Language Acquisition

Belasco	Rivers		Valette
Pre-Nucleation	Skill-Getting:	Cognition Production (Pseudo- Communication)	I. Mechanical Skills II. Knowledge III. Transfer
Nucleation			
Post-Nucleation	Skill-Using:	Interaction	IV. Communication
Mastery			

is to enable the teacher to analyze the types of items he uses on his tests. Our standard tests, by their very nature, measure almost uniquely activities in the areas of Mechanical Skills, Knowledge and Transfer. This is because test items in which there is one correct predictable answer are mainly measures of phonology, vocabulary and structure. Certain listening and reading comprehension tests do measure the student's ability to understand authentic materials, but all too often the items based on these passages show a heavy vocabulary bias, that is, the student who knows the meaning of a specific word will answer the item correctly, whereas the student who does not, cannot from the context discover the meaning of that word. Since free speaking and free writing tests cannot be scored with 100% reliability, they usually do not figure on standard tests.

Our classroom tests reveal similar preoccupations: we check the students' pronunciation and spelling, we give vocabulary and grammar quizzes of various sorts. What happens to communication? All too often it is paid mere lip service: what really "counts" is student performance on tests in the areas of "pre-nucleation" or "skill-getting."

There seem to be two interrelated explanations why students who study a foreign language in the classroom environment generally fail to reach the goal of "genuine communication" which Imhoof so heavily stressed. The first is that teachers do not teach it and the second is that teachers do not test it. And the reason most teachers do not teach or test communication is that they do not know how to do it. Some of them never really learned how to communicate themselves. And those who do feel comfortable with the language they teach, generally acquired this communication by residing in the country where that language is spoken, or else speak it natively. I am convinced that most teachers tend to teach the way they themselves were taught, and hence it is not at all surprising that since the teachers were never formally taught communication skills in the classroom, they themselves are poorly equipped to do so now.

What I propose to do today, is to make some specific suggestions about how to teach and test communication skills. Although my official topic is evaluation, one can hardly speak meaningfully about the classroom testing of communication skills without touching on the matter of teaching techniques. The form which the skills tests take are self-evident: to test whether a student can talk in a foreign language, you have him talk. To test whether he can understand a newscast, you play a newscast for him. To test whether he can read a newspaper article, you give him a newspaper article. What is tricky is bringing him to the point where he can indeed perform, and then evaluating the quality of his performance. Actually, these two things often go together.

First let me go back to an experience of my own. Several years ago I was assigned a class in a multi-section course entitled "Composition and Conversation." Our basic materials were an audio-lingual review grammar and a reader. The trouble with the review grammar was that it focused on the complexities of the language, whereas many of my students were unsure of the basics. But the oral drills were lively and the class responded well. The reader contained stories so abstract that most students would have had trouble understanding them in their native language, and most of our "conversation" consisted of my asking factual questions and the students answering them to the best of their ability. At the end of the semester I gave a "speaking" test. Each student stood in front of the class and gave a prepared talk—without notes—about a topic of his choice. I have not forgotten the ensuing scene, which, with a couple of rare exceptions, went like this: The "victim" stood at the front of the room, head bowed, and rapidly muttered his talk. I patiently strained my ears to try to grasp what he was saying and judge its grammaticality. No one else was paying attention. Why should they have? The "talks" were quite incomprehensible, for the students were not trying to communicate. Those who had already spoken were bored. Those whose turn was approaching were nervous. I realized then that these students were *unable* to communicate in the foreign language, but also that the failure was mine for I had not taught them that skill. The course emphasis had been on pre-nucleation aspects of learning, on skill-getting and not skill-using, on mechanical skills, acquisition of knowledge and transfer activities in the forms of drills and exercises. Genuine communication was neither taught, nor tested.

Performance on the "composition" part of the examination, though less trying on the students from a psychological point of view, was equally lamentable. But here, too, I was to blame, for we surely had not concentrated on written self-expression in the class either. In fact, I had fallen into a rather common trap which consists of spending classtime in teacher directed question-answer activities, assigning some written exercises and drills for homework, and then expecting, quite naively, that the skill of writing paragraphs or essays has mysteriously entered the students' heads so that they can produce effectively a short composition on a final examination.

As for the skills of reading and listening, I am sure my students could hardly do either. Not only did I not train them how to read material or how to understand the spoken language (aside from having them plow laboriously through the aforementioned stories and listen to my statements or the models on the exercise tapes in the laboratory), but I never tested it.

Let me share with you now some of my subsequent experiences in teaching and testing communication.[7]

Speaking. It is self-evident that if the teacher wants the students to learn to speak another language, he must give them the opportunity to do so and must motivate them so that they will indeed wish to do so. This means that the teacher must learn to listen and must devise a variety of small-group activities for the students. If you have 24 students and a period of 50 minutes and if, as a teacher, you ask questions and the students respond, then you are talking half of the time (or more, if you elaborate on your questions, which most teachers are wont to do). At best, the students have 25 minutes to talk, which averages out to one minute per student. This you will readily admit is not very much. However, if you divide your class into groups of four students, then each student will have an average of ten minutes to talk, and moreover he will be actively listening for the rest of the time, since in a group of four people he cannot very well let his mind wander. As a teacher, you move from group to group, listening in, occasionally answering questions, and taking notes on the kind of mistakes the students are making. If you then use ten minutes at the end of the period to go over some of these errors, the students will be receptive, for you are treating precisely those aspects of phonology, vocabulary and syntax which were troubling them.

The speaking activities must of course be structured, especially at first when students feel quite hesitant about expressing themselves orally. With my more advanced classes, the point of departure is usually a provocative essay. The outside preparation consists of two parts. First the student must write down three new words or expressions, define them in the foreign language (preferably with the help of a dictionary), and use each in an original sentence. This is to encourage him to build his personal vocabulary. Second, he prepares two or three questions based on the reading. When we first begin this type of activity, I have the entire class move their chairs into a circle. Then I have one student read a question. He is directed to ask this question of someone in the class. That person at first usually responds with "Could you please repeat the question?" When all those who want to respond to the questions have, another student is called on to ask the following question. During this full-class activity, the students review the interrogative forms, and also learn that opinion questions are much more likely to arouse reactions than simple factual questions. As the teacher, I do not correct mistakes, since I do not want to inhibit their responses. Nor do I answer their questions about "How do you say this or that?" but rather have them ask a classmate for help or work out a paraphrase in the foreign language. After two or three class periods, I find that I can break up the class into small groups and that each group can easily maintain a discussion for half an hour. Students also feel freer in the small groups and are less hesitant about expressing themselves than they were before a large group. At the end of the term the student's ability to discuss a prepared text is tested in an interview session. His performance is rated on a scale of 1 to 5 in areas such as comprehensibility, ability to respond to questions, and fluency, as well as appropriateness of vocabulary, accuracy in use of structure, and pronunciation.

In the conversation class, the self-expression activities are not solely limited to small group discussion of texts. We also engage in full-class debates, impromptu skits based on listening materials heard in the lab, round-robin activities in which one group prepares a question which the next group has to answer, etc.

During the term, the students are graded on the regularity of their classroom preparation and their degree of participation in conversation activities. By placing the emphasis on communication rather than accuracy, I find the students are more motivated to speak. The ensuing increase in amount of speaking usually leads of itself to a higher degree of accuracy in expression.

In addition to communication activities, it is necessary that the course include means of improving the student's command of the elements of the language (skill-getting activities).

a. Pronunciation. The students work on their own with laboratory tapes. As a test, they record fifteen sentences. I listen to each recording and grade it as follows: Two or fewer pronunciation mistakes on the entire group of sentences: A; three or more mistakes: F. The students retake the test until they pass it. Since all students are given the opportunity of attaining an A, there is a certain motivation to retake the test until they can pronounce the sentences accurately. While there is not necessarily an immediate carry-over into the conversation activities (that is, students can correct a pronunciation problem on the tape while they are concentrating on it, but will make the same mistakes once more in a free conversation where their attention is on what they are saying rather than how they are saying it), the students do all realize that by the end of the course they indeed control the phonology of the language they are learning.

b. Verb forms. Although all of my French students know that a singular subject takes a singular verb and a plural subject takes a plural verb, many tend to use a singular verb with a plural subject. For regular -er verbs, the singular and plural forms generally sound the same, but for most other verbs there is a difference in pronunciation. I have discovered that many students do not "hear" the difference between singular and plural forms, and hence do not make the distinctions when they speak. Here again, their effort is concentrated on the content of the message they are trying to get across, and not on its form. As an exercise, I frequently read lists of sentences which the students must identify as being singular or plural. This type of selective listening can easily be tested in the same way it is taught. Retest opportunities should be made available to the students.

c. Vocabulary. Vocabulary building activities grow out of the readings and the discussion topics. Since the words selected are immediately used in conversation, the students tend to retain them. Vocabulary growth can be tested in a traditional way, again allowing students to take tests over to improve their grades.

d. Grammatical patterns. During the speaking activities, I, as the teacher, note those structures which prove difficult. If the problem is generalized, I present the structure to the full class. If only certain students have difficulty with a structure, I have those students review it outside of class, or I take them aside. A good deal of structure review takes place as a result of the student's written preparation for class. In addition, my students are assigned pattern-type grammar exercises in the laboratory. Several times during the term, I give oral grammar tests based on these recorded exercises. The quizzes consist of four vocabulary words to be defined and four items from the exercises. If the student defines a word correctly, he receives 2 points. If he defines that word incorrectly but can give the right meaning on the second try, he gets 1 point. If he fails the second time, he receives 0. For each drill item, I read the model and then the cue sentence. If the student answers correctly, he gets 4 points. If he gets the grammatical transformation right, but makes some minor error, or hesitates a great deal, he gets 3 points. If he gives the wrong response, and can correct it easily, he receives 2 points. If he corrects his error but makes some minor mistake or hesitates a great deal, he receives 1 point. If he does not produce the right answer on the second try, he gets 0. The maximum score for each quiz is 24 points. Grades are awarded as follows: 22 to 24 points, A; 20-21 points, B; 17-19 points, C; 15-16 points, D; 14 or below, F. The student may take the test over to improve his grade.

You will have noted that the tests and activities in the conversation class I have been describing are of two sorts: those at the taxonomical stage of communication, which corresponds to Rivers' skill-using level, and those at the lower taxonomical stages which correspond to the skill-getting level.

For the communication activities, the main concerns are developing student motivation to speak and increasing fluency and ease of expression. Immediate correction of errors is avoided for it might inhibit student desire to speak. Student performance is simply evaluated in terms of participation and general comprehensibility.

For the activities which focus on the improvement of pronunciation, the development of vocabulary and the accuracy of structure, the teacher's concern is to improve the student's command of the elements of the language. The traditional testing and grading system in which a test is given only once and students are graded A, B, C, etc., tends to favor those students with a good grammar background. The students who most need the help, that is, those with a weak background, are discouraged, because they quickly realize that even if they work very hard, the better students with hardly any studying will get the good grades. A test-retest system in which several retests are available and in which only the student's highest grade is recorded encourages all students to study seriously. An A or B is within reach of everyone who is willing to expend the effort. I have found, in fact, that although I have raised my standards for honor marks, the students attain these grades in greater numbers because now the system rewards their efforts.

Writing. In many ways, the teaching and testing of the written skill and of the speaking skill are similar. In order to teach written self-expression, the majority of the classroom time should be spent on the writing and analysis of paragraphs and essays, while development of vocabulary and the mastery of structure and spelling should be relegated outside the regular classroom via programmed materials, review grammars, self-correcting workbooks, and the like. Specific or lexical problems which come up in the context of a particular writing activity can, of course, be treated in the classroom. The testing of spelling, vocabulary and structure can be carried out with short quizzes given on a test-retest basis: this approach parallels that described with respect to speaking. Most teachers have a variety of means of testing these aspects of language learning. Standard tests, teaching programs and handbooks abound in examples of item types.

Let us concentrate on the communication aspect of writing. As was the case in the teaching of speaking, there are two features which must be kept in mind. First, the student must be motivated to wish to express himself in writing. Second, he needs sufficient practice in written self-expression. Traditionally, teachers have killed off student motivation by using red pencil to mark every minor spelling error. The emphasis on form took all attention away from the content of the writing. Students also quickly learned that simple but accurate sentences were more acceptable than more complex sentences into which some errors might creep. In other words, creativity was usually stifled. The writing skill has further suffered from lack of training. Now it is obvious to any practicing teacher that if thirty students write essays every day, this represents many hours per night spent in correcting them. Furthermore, if a teacher has four or five classes of thirty students each, the ensuing preparation time is overwhelming. What might the teacher do to improve the writing skill of his students, while at the same time preserving his sanity?

One way of giving students opportunity to write a great deal and yet to reduce the correcting time is to assign group compositions. If twenty-five students each write for half an hour, they produce twenty-five rather long compositions. But if these students work in groups of five, they produce only five compositions. (Each student, however, writes out his own copy, so that all group members are directly involved in the activity.) The first advantage is that the class produces only one-fifth the number of papers. Secondly, it usually happens that what one student has forgotten, another student still remembers: hence the resulting group composition will be more accurate than a composition written by any of its members individually. Third, since the teacher moves around the class during the writing, he answers some questions and corrects some faulty structures before they are written down in the final draft. Fourth, since students discuss each sentence before writing it, within a thirty-minute period they will write less than an individual working alone would have produced. Finally, the students will have been talking to each other in the foreign language: an added bonus in the area of oral expression. At the end of the hour, each group could write its composition on a ditto master. At the next class meeting, each student would receive the five compositions produced by the class. These could then be evaluated by the students themselves. Since no individual's work is being dissected (group work breeds anonymity) the students do not fear being critical and objective in expressing their opinions. The class might be asked to rank the compositions in order of preference. Next, the students would be asked to describe which qualities they think characterize a good composition. The class might come up with categories such as: organization, good opening sentence, appropriate use of vocabulary, original imagery, etc. Once this list of characteristics has been established (and is written on the board or on an overhead transparency), the class looks over each composition once more and rates it on the scale. Let us suppose that for each category 5 points means very good, 3 points average, and 1 point poor. After this evaluation, the total points for each composition are tallied. Hopefully, the composition rated "best" by the class has the highest number of points, while the poorest composition has the lowest number. If this is indeed the case, then the rating scale has been unofficially "validated." If not, the class might discuss whether they wish to modify their original ranking or whether they feel that some important characteristics have been omitted from their rating scale. Maybe they think that some characteristics on their scale are more important than others and they would like to assign them twice or three times the number of points: for example, 15 points for very good; 9 points for average, and 3 points for poor. By the end of the period, the class will have worked out an acceptable rating grid.

At a later date, when an actual writing test is given, the teacher could use the rating scale established by the class to grade the papers. This technique is of motivational value for several reasons. The students find the system to be more objective, and hence fairer, since they have participated in its design and modification. Secondly, each student knows on which basis his essay will be graded and can try to improve it along specified guidelines.

As in the case of speaking activities, not all written work must be graded. Much benefit is derived from the practice of writing. One technique is to have the students keep a daily logbook. They would be graded simply on the regularity of the entries or perhaps, if necessary, on the variety of structures and sentence types used. This latter restriction will encourage students to write more than simply "Nothing happened today."

Another technique is to have students, either singly or in pairs, compose their own answers to "Dear Abby" or similar requests for advice. This type of activity could be combined with conversation practice in which each group reads its answers aloud to the others.

Another combined writing-speaking activity consists in the preparation of short skits. Students in pairs or in groups of three or four prepare a script of two pages or so. For example, they may prepare a commercial for an imaginary product or a travelogue designed to induce the listener to visit an area where the language is spoken. The teacher circulates to help groups with their projects. At the end, each group can give its skit in front of the class. If facilities permit, the skits may be videotaped. In the latter case, a special script must be prepared with the text in one column and the directions to the camera crew in a facing column. Once each group has videotaped their presentation, the entire class sees the composite videotape. As an additional writing project, the tape may be viewed a second time during which each student takes notes. These notes are then written up in the form of short resumés for the next class meeting.

The creative teacher can think up a variety of writing projects at the level of communication. In writing, as in speaking, the main aim of instruction is to create an open environment where students feel free to express themselves. Grades would be given for participation and creative use of language.

Listening. Of the four communication skills, that of listening comprehension is probably least taught in the classroom and least tested. Although a certain amount of time is devoted to skill-getting activities, such as sound discrimination (mechanical skills), oral vocabulary and structure drills (knowledge), and listening to the teacher and classmates using the known forms in new combinations (transfer), very little time is spent training the students to understand the language as it is spoken in the "real world." Of course, in small group conversation activities, the students do pay attention to what their classmates are saying, and this is, in a sense, the first step in listening comprehension. But we usually do not teach them how to understand foreign language radio programs, television shows, films, lectures, rapid conversations among speakers of the language. We almost never give classroom tests of listening comprehension, although the wide availability of tapes, videotapes and films would make it easy to do so. In fact, listening comprehension seems to be the one communication skill that teachers feel is best taught in the foreign environment and has no place in the classroom. The native teacher of the foreign language has been brought up to believe that reading and writing are the important skills and tends to slight listening comprehension. The nonnative teacher of the language has perhaps not acquired a high level of listening comprehension himself and feels uneasy in front of a rapid flow of language.

The teaching of listening comprehension and the testing of that skill are closely linked. Listening comprehension is an activity which takes place within the head of the student. In order to determine whether the student has understood what he has heard, the teacher must resort to indirect evaluation: questions on what has been heard (true-false items, multiple-choice questions, open-ended questions), oral or written resumés by the student, native language equivalents, or written transcriptions. The type of techniques used will, of course, vary depending on the aims of the teacher and the level of the class.

It seems to be at the beginning levels of language learning that listening comprehension activities are most needed, and usually omitted altogether. If students are only presented with slow, carefully enunciated forms of the foreign language, they feel completely lost when they later come into contact with normal speech. They do not know how to cope with the rapid flow of unfamiliar language. In our beginning classes we can let students spend a few minutes each period hearing language they do not entirely understand. At first, the teacher might relate incidents that happened to him or narrate a story using pictures. (It is often possible to find a folk tale that is common to the student's native language and retell it in the foreign language.) Newscasts of current events may be introduced early in the course. At first students will only grasp a few words, but gradually their comprehension will increase. Newscasts may also be assigned as listening comprehension work in the language laboratory.

At the intermediate level, students may listen to radio plays or dramatizations, for which no script is made available. This semester at Boston College in our French conversation classes we used a James-Bond type dramatization in 24 episodes entitled *Suivez la Piste.* [8] The students listened to the series in the laboratory as homework and answered true-false questions on each episode in their notebooks. False statements had to be rectified. As a follow-up speaking activity, we occasionally did impromptu skits in class based on the episodes they had been listening to. Sometimes the student gave oral resumés! The final episode of the series can be considered a test, and the students graded on their performance in the recorded true-false test. As a more precise comprehension check, the teacher can play portions of the tape in class, stopping it after each sentence, and asking students to give a rapid native-language equivalent. This type of activity forces students to listen more carefully to exactly what is being said. When the students are trying to get the gist of the recording, they first listen for the content words: the nouns, verbs, adjectives. When forced to provide native-language equivalents, the students must pay attention to structural markers. Was the subject singular or plural? Did the action take place in the present or the past? etc. As a testing device, students may be asked to write down the native-language equivalent, or to choose the best among three possible native-language equivalents in the multiple-choice format.

The most demanding type of listening-comprehension activity is that of written transcriptions.[9] The recordings can be radio broadcasts, speeches, recorded conversations, or the sound tracks of films or television programs. The student works independently with a tape or a cassette at a machine which allows him to stop and replay segments he wants to hear again. As out-of-class preparation, he writes down in the foreign language exactly what he hears. In class, each student puts a different sentence on the board and the period is spent having the students themselves correct the text as best they can. The lexical, phonological and syntactical problems of the text are discussed. The students do many of these transcriptions during the course, and thereby prepare themselves for the test which is an unfamiliar transcription. I usually let the students do the test transcriptions over the period of a week and allow them to use whatever reference books they wish to. The only restriction is that they not talk to each other about their work.

There are many possible variations on the transcription technique. For example, the teacher may distribute a list of difficult words and expressions which occur in the text. The teacher may prepare two or three forms of the transcriptions for students of varying abilities: the best student must write the entire transcription. The average student receives a ditto sheet in which some of the key expressions are listed in the order in which they occur. The weaker students may be given a partial text in which they fill in the blanks.

Our language laboratory permits two sets of headphones to be jacked into each cassette recorder. This means that those students who so desire can prepare the transcription in pairs. In a recent article, Paul Carstens describes a technique for group transcriptions.[10] Five or six students listen to the same tape via headphones and a jack box. On each sentence they must come to a complete consensus before each person writes it out and are only allowed to speak the foreign language during this activity. In arriving at a consensus, group dynamics play an important role. As the case for group speaking activities described earlier, grades, if they must be assigned, should be awarded on the basis of participation as well as on the accuracy of the resulting transcription.

Reading. There is a great deal of literature available on the teaching of the reading skill, and the field is much too vast for me to presume to review it in a few minutes. The standard tests in foreign languages all contain reading selections of the following general format: an unfamiliar reading followed by multiple-choice comprehension questions. Although some of these tests suffer from a vocabulary bias, that is, although many of these tests have a high proportion of items which measure whether or not the student knows a specific word or expression, it is nonetheless true that many items test general comprehension and inference techniques.

Our concern here is how the teacher can best test reading in the classroom. As was the case with listening, reading comprehension is also an activity which takes place within the head of the students and which the teacher measures indirectly through questions, resumés, and translations. Yet while all teachers know how to read with some degree of fluency, and although they all know what forms reading tests can take, very few teachers actually give reading tests in class. Generally the teacher gives a written test of some sort (questions, resumés, interpretations) *based* on a prior reading selection which has been read and discussed in class. Although reading has occurred in preparation for the test, the skill of reading is not measured in such a test. Rather, the student demonstrates his ability to retain facts and to organize them appropriately.

To measure how well a student can *read* a foreign language, we must give him an unfamiliar passage as part of the test. It is most appropriate if this passage is similar in style and content to material he has been reading in class. For example, if students of English have been reading articles in *Time* magazine, then the reading on the test should be a new article from an unfamiliar issue of *Time*. Comprehension can be checked with short-answer questions. Before closing, let me briefly describe one way of preparing students for standard reading tests by using the sample materials which appear in the books designed to prepare students for such tests. The reading passage and its items are put on three overhead transparencies. The first contains the reading passage. The second contains the stem or the opening line of the test items. The third contains the four multiple-choice options. The three transparencies are prepared so that if placed one on top of the other they reconstitute the reading test as it appears in the book. These transparencies are used as follows. First the students are shown only the passage. The teacher asks questions about the difficult expressions, the general theme, and the information contained in the reading. Then he puts the second transparency on the overhead, so that the students can see the passage and the stems of the questions. Students offer completions and responses to these stems. Finally the multiple-choice options are placed on the overhead projector, and the students determine which option is the most appropriate choice. Through this type of classroom practice, the students learn how to read a passage, how to infer meanings of words from context, and how to determine the appropriate answers to reading comprehension questions.

Developing genuine communication skills within the constraints of the classroom environment is the foremost challenge to the language teacher. The elements of language, the phonology, the lexicon and the structures, can be acquired from books, tapes, programmed materials and the like. But their acquisition does not automatically lead to communicative competence. Communication must be nurtured and taught. By stressing listening comprehension, reading comprehension, and self-expression via speaking and writing, and by evaluating student progress in these skills, the teacher will strengthen his language program while satisfying the needs of his students.

NOTES

1. Maurice Imhoof, 1973. "Foreword," *TESOL Quarterly* 7: 1, 2.

2. Simon Belasco. 1965. "Nucleation and the audio-lingual approach," *Modern Language Journal* XLIX: 8, 482-491.

3. Wilga M. Rivers, 1972. "Talking off the tops of their heads," *TESOL Quarterly* 6: 1, 71-81. Also reprinted in Rivers, *Speaking in Many Tongues: Essays in Foreign-Language Teaching.* Expanded 2d Edition. Rowley, Mass.: Newbury House, 1976.

4. For the most recent taxonomy see Rebecca M. Valette and Renée S. Disick, 1972. *Modern Language Performance Objectives and Individualization: A Handbook.* New York: Harcourt, Brace, Jovanovich, chapter 2.

5. Simon Belasco, 1967. "The Plateau; or the case for comprehension: the 'Concept' Approach," *Modern Language Journal* LI: 2, pp. 82-88.

6. Wilga M. Rivers, 1973. "From linguistic competence to communicative competence," *TESOL Quarterly* 7: 1, pp. 25-34.

7. See also Rebecca M. Valette, 1967. *Modern Language Testing: A Handbook.* New York: Harcourt Brace & World; and Edward D. Allen and Rebecca M. Valette, 1972. *Modern Language Classroom Techniques: A Handbook.* New York: Harcourt, Brace, Jovanovich.

8. Distributed by EMC Corporation, 180 East 6th Street, St. Paul, Minnesota 55101. Produced by British Broadcasting Corporation.

9. See Belasco, "The Plateau . . ." pp. 87-88.

10. Paul Carstens, 1973. "Small-group listening-transcription: path to a new dimension in foreign language learning?" *American Foreign Language Teacher* 3: 3, 32-33.

TOPICS FOR DISCUSSION AND/OR ACTION RESEARCH

"MOI TARZAN, VOUS JANE?
A STUDY OF COMMUNICATIVE COMPETENCE"

by *Patricia B. Westphal*

1. Set up an interview similar to the one conducted by Westphal for one of your classes. Use your own textbook materials to draw up your bits of information. Perhaps another language teacher or a native speaker in your community can help you with this. Try to categorize the errors made by your students. Can you trace the cause of any of them to your teaching strategies?

2. See Bonin and Birckbichler's "Real Communication through Conversation and Interview Cards" and Joiner's "Self-Directed Dialogue: A Technique for Conversational Practice" (see Part II) for ways to use the interview situation as a teaching technique.

3. Westphal suggests that "... it is possible that correction in terms of communication requirements might be more fruitful than any other kind, since this seems to be important to students." What implications does this remark have for the correction of gender errors, tense errors, and lexical errors?

4. Would a native speaker of the language you teach be more severe or less severe than you are in judging the speech of your students? If you have contact with native speakers, ask them to rank from least irritating to most irritating at least five errors made by your students. Which of these errors interfere most with understanding?

5. Belasco, as quoted by Westphal, suggests that only a limited number of structures be practiced for active use. Examine the grammatical points included in your textbook and decide which should be taught for active use and which for passive recognition only.

"TEACHING FOR COMMUNICATION"

by *Sandra J. Savignon*

1. Is contextualized language practice such as that described by Palmer and Slager adequate to preparing students for unrehearsed, real-life situations such as those described by Savignon, or is some specific training in coping strategies necessary?

2. Follow Savignon's suggestion and talk to your students about what it means to communicate in a second language. Can you add questions of your own to the ones she suggests? Make a list of insights you gain from this discussion. How can they help you to be a more effective teacher?

3. Compare the position of Savignon toward "mistakes" or "errors" in oral production with that of Paulston and Selekman. Should error correction strategies be the same whether the student is participating in skill-getting or skill-using activities? What is the relationship between error correction and general classroom atmosphere?

4. What are the equivalents to "whatchamacallit," "thing," "tool," "machine," etc., in the language you teach? List these, and then use them to describe a can opener, a sewing machine, a vacuum cleaner, a garden hose, an electric blanket. Try out a similar exercise with your students. Take notes and analyze your results.

5. After carefully preparing them to expect some frustration, try giving your students a communication task that is beyond their linguistic capabilities. For example, before the students have learned to tell time in the foreign language, ask one person in each pair to find out when his partner's mother or father arrives home from work. The only restriction is that English must not be used. Note student reactions to this task.

6. Do you use the foreign language to give your assignments, conduct exercises, etc., in class? Record one of your classes and then listen to the tape to determine how much authentic communication or real language use took place during the class.

"STRUCTURAL PATTERN DRILLS: A CLASSIFICATION"

by *Christina Bratt Paulston*

1. Paulston points out that at the mechanical level the student can ignore the meaning of the language being manipulated. Can you think of any advantages in trying to encourage students to think about meaning, even in drills at this level? What justification for the use of mechanical drills does Paulston give?

2. Cite an example from your own experience that illustrates students' failure to transfer to communicative situations the skills learned in mechanical drills.

3. Beyond the mechanical level, Paulston's examples of meaningful and communicative drills consist of question-and-answer practice. Will her classification apply to role-playing, gaming, simulation, etc.?

4. Discuss the four-skill fusion approach or the use of conversation cards (see Part II) in light of Paulston's quote from Francis Johnson, "Communication requires interpersonal responsiveness, rather than the mere production of language which is truthful, honest, accurate, stylistically pleasing, etc."

5. Paulston states that the essential distinction between "a meaningful drill and a communicative drill is that the latter adds *new* information about the *real* world." This definition of communication and the one cited in number four above may imply very different kinds of student responses. Which definition is more appropriate to your needs?

"INTERACTION ACTIVITIES IN THE FOREIGN LANGUAGE CLASSROOM, OR HOW TO GROW A TULIP-ROSE"

by *Christina Bratt Paulston* and *Howard R. Selekman*

1. The next time you conduct an oral drill, substitute a nonsense word as a test of whether your students are aware of the meaning of the words they are saying.

2. Using the example supplied by Paulston and Selekman as a model, design a series of activities (Stage 1 through Stage 3) to practice one or

more of the following points of grammar: adjective agreement, the past tense, negation.

3. Try one of the interaction activities described by Paulston and Selekman with your students. Take note of the most serious errors that occur and design drills to practice the imperfectly learned grammatical constructions.

4. Make a list of people in your community who might be willing to cooperate in an activity similar to "Direct Line to Hebrew." In addition to native speakers, there may be retired language teachers who would really enjoy such an opportunity. Would you want to tell your students that they would be speaking with people who knew no English? If not, do you think the activity could still be worthwhile?

5. Paulston and Selekman stress the importance of peer teaching in interaction activities. Observe your students as they work together and try to determine which of them are most successful at peer teaching. Group your students to make the most of their talents.

"SKILL-USING, SELF-EXPRESSION AND COMMUNICATION: EXERCISES IN THREE DIMENSIONS"

by *Sidney N. J. Zelson*

1. Zelson lists 9 features which skill-using exercises should include. Examine the interview and conversation card technique (Bonin and Birchbickler, Pt. II), the fusion technique (Kalivoda, Elkins, Morain, Pt. II), and the strip-story (Gibson, Pt. II) to see which of these features are, or could be, included in each.

2. Paulston states that to be truly communicative an activity should add new information about the real world. Consider expanded sentences as described by Zelson from this point of view. Would you classify this activity as mechanical, meaningful or communicative?

3. Zelson gives 3 examples of the monologue format. For which level is each appropriate? To check your answer, try these or similar monologue activities with your students.

4. In his examples of two and three dimensional activities (a–j), the only two activities which lack the third dimension, i.e., focus on a particular grammatical structure, are role-playing activities. How do you explain this? Would it be possible to create a three-dimensional role-play activity?

5. In Zelson's implied definition, communicative competence does not necessarily require linguistic competence. Gestures and a few vocabulary items can make a minimal kind of communication possible. What weight do you/would you like to give to each of the components of Zelson's "proficiency" construct?

"TEACHING COMMUNICATION"

by *Adrian Palmer*

1. Both Palmer and Slager make general observations about the textbook and its effect on classroom practice. Compare their attitudes, then review your own text in light of their suggestions. Does your text, for example, introduce question patterns quickly as Palmer recommends?

2. Paulston classifies oral language practice as mechanical, meaningful, or communicative. Rivers, as quoted by Paulston and Selekman, views language practice as consisting of skill-using or skill-getting activities. How do you think each of them would categorize Palmer's examples of communication practice drills? Give reasons for your point of view.

3. Palmer takes the sentence "I would tell him to shut the door" and analyzes the structural elements that students will have to deal with in order to participate in a drill based on that sentence. Take a comparable sentence in the language you teach and analyze it as the basis of a drill. Try out such a drill with actual students to test the accuracy of your analysis.

4. Palmer stresses the importance of exposing students to language that is situationally as well as grammatically correct and Slager has pointed out that teachers sometimes ask students to produce language that would not occur in real-life situations. Have you observed usage in the classroom that would be judged socially inappropriate and/or unrealistic by a native speaker of the language? List several examples.

5. Create a verbal context for drilling agreement of adjectives, limiting the student response you expect to the linguistic elements your students will already have mastered.

6. Palmer suggests using comprehensibility as the criterion for choosing which errors in pronunciation to correct. Record a sample of student speech and try to listen to it as a native speaker would. Rank at

least 5 of the student's errors according to the threat they pose to comprehension.

7. In this technique what is the ratio of student talk to teacher talk? of native language use to target language use? What conclusions do you draw from your analysis?

"CREATING CONTEXTS FOR LANGUAGE PRACTICE"

by *William R. Slager*

1. Evaluate Palmer's communication practice drills in light of Slager's recommendations for teaching language in realistic contexts.

2. Criticize the following exercise by applying Slager's ten assumptions about contextualization to it. Imagine that the exercise occurs in a workbook designed to accompany a text for teaching English to adolescents.

A Birthday Party   Mary's four-year-old sister Anne is very greedy and besides, this is her birthday. Whenever Mary offers her a portion of any of the refreshments she says she wants all of the food or beverage in question. Write Anne's responses to Mary's questions.

> *Model*   Mary: Would you like some lemonade?
> Anne: Yes, I want it all.

1. Mary: Would you like some ice cream?
   Anne:
2. Mary: Would you like some peanuts?
   Anne:
3. Mary: Would you like some cake?
   Anne:
4. Mary: Would you like some mints?
   Anne:
5. Mary: Would you like some cookies?
   Anne:

3. Slager says that the language teacher should be a collector of contexts. What circumstances in the real world would be likely to evoke the use of conditional statements, possessive pronouns, the present participle and the passive voice in the language you teach? Use your findings to create drills based on specific contexts for these structures.

"DEVELOPING AND EVALUATING COMMUNICATION SKILLS IN THE CLASSROOM"

by *Rebecca M. Valette*

1. Belasco's theoretical construct implies that the student must learn a considerable amount of structure before s/he is able to begin to develop communication skills. Paulston and Selekman, on the other hand, have stressed the importance of communicative interaction in the early weeks of language study. Considering Valette's analogy of learning to ski, which of these positions would she be likely to take? Where do *you* stand?

2. For one of the classes you teach make a table of the approximate percentage of time your students spend working at each level of Valette's taxonomy. Then review your most recent test and enter the percentage of formal evaluation you have included for each level. Does your testing program encourage the goal of communication?

3. Consider the criteria of Valette's rating scale for oral practice. Which of the criteria focus on linguistic competence and which on communicative competence? If you used this scale, would you weigh any of the items more heavily than others?

4. Would you classify the small group question-answer sessions Valette describes as communicative drill or communicative interaction as the terms are used by Paulston and Selekman? How would you evaluate the students' regularity of classroom preparation and degree of participation?

5. As Valette points out, many speaking and listening activities can be adapted for use in developing writing and reading skills. Transform at least one of the activities from the second section of this book for use as a communicative exercise in reading and another for writing.

6. What value do you see, if any, in giving students experience in listening to samples of the foreign language which you don't expect them to understand very well?

7. Where in her taxonomy would you classify Valette's suggestions for using written transcriptions? How would you evaluate them? What role would spelling play?

8. From Rivers' list of the normal purposes of language (see "Interaction Activities in the Foreign Classroom, or How to Grow a Tulip-Rose"), develop one activity for evaluation purposes. Include directions to the students and the method you would use for assigning grades.

SUGGESTED ADDITIONAL READING

Holley, Freda M., and Janet K. King. "Imitation and Correction in Foreign Language Learning." *Modern Language Journal,* 55 (1971), 494-498.

Contains specific suggestions for dealing constructively with student errors in oral language practice.

Jarvis, Gilbert A. "Testing for Meaning and Communication in the Foreign Language Classroom." (Paper delivered at meeting of Wisconsin Association of Foreign Language Teachers.) (EDRS: ED 123-886).

Contrasts traditional test questions with others which test the communication of meaningful content.

Jarvis, Gilbert A. and William N. Hatfield. "The Practice Variable: An Experiment." *Foreign Language Annals,* 4 (1971), 401-410.

Results indicate that contextualized language practice which consistently requires students to "tell the truth" increases their ability to speak and to write French.

Joiner, Elizabeth G. "Communicative versus Non-Communicative Language Practice in the Teaching of Beginning College French." *Modern Language Journal,* 61 (1977), 236-242.

An experimental study which indicates that practice in transmission and reception of messages enables students to perform better in situations which call for real language use.

Oller, John W. Jr. "Linguistics and the Pragmatics of Communication." (Paper presented at the fourth annual TESOL Convention, San Francisco, 1970.) (EDRS: ED 041-292.)

Criticizes the transformational approach to language. Argues that all language must be studied within the context of communication.

Oller, John W. Jr., and Dean H. Obrecht. "Pattern Drill and Communicative Activity: A Psycholinguistic Experiment." *IRAL,* 6 (1968), 165-174.

Results suggest that practicing language patterns in context improves retention and general learning of structures.

Oller, John W. Jr., and Jack C. Richards, eds. *Focus on the Learner.* Rowley, Mass.: Newbury House, 1973.

A selection of articles representing many aspects of the psychology of second-language learning and the student as a variable in this learning. Of particular interest are Parts II, III, and IV which deal with language learning processes, error analysis, and oral testing.

Palmer, Adrian S. "Testing Communication." *IRAL,* 10 (1972), 35-45.

Research report on the development of a test of oral communication proficiency.

Paulston, Christina Bratt. "Linguistic and Communicative Competence." *TESOL Quarterly,* 8 (1974), 347-362.

Stresses the importance to accurate communication of knowledge of social conventions. Gives a sample lesson plan for providing manipulative, meaningful and communicative practice.

Rivers, Wilga M. "The Natural and the Normal in Language Teaching: Where's the Difference?" In *Personalizing Language Instruction: Learning Styles and Teaching Options.* Ed. R.A. Schulz. Skokie, Ill.: National Textbook, 1977, pp. 101-108.

Distinctions are drawn between what is natural and what is normal in language use. Functions of language are discussed and related to classroom language practice.

Rivers, Wilga M. *Speaking in Many Tongues: Essays in Foreign-Language Teaching,* expanded 2nd edition. Rowley, Mass.: Newbury House, 1976.

Of special interest are "Talking Off the Tops of Their Heads," which contains the skill-getting, skill-using model, and "From Linguistic Competence to Communicative Competence," which elaborates this distinction.

Savignon, Sandra J. *Communicative Competence: An Experiment in Foreign Language Teaching.* Philadelphia: Center for Curriculum Development, 1972.

Report of an experiment which indicates that linguistic competence and communicative competence are distinct but related constructs. Includes examples of tests of communicative competence and suggestions for scoring.

Schumann, John H., and Nancy Stenson, eds. *New Frontiers in Second Language Learning.* Rowley, Mass.: Newbury House, 1974.

Treats especially the idea that errors are evidence of learning strategies of second-language learners. Contains both practical and theoretical articles.

Schulz, Renate A. "Discrete-Point versus Simulated Communication Testing in Foreign Languages." *Modern Language Journal,* 61 (1977), 94-101.

Distinguishes between the two types of tests and suggests that if communicative ability is the major aim of instruction, simulated communication tests tend to increase this kind of achievement.

Schulz, Renate A., ed. *Teaching for Communication in the Foreign Language Classroom.* Skokie, Ill.: National Textbook, 1976.

Contains five articles specifically dealing with communication. Theory, classroom techniques and testing are included.

Schulz, Renate A., and Walter H. Bartz. "Free to Communicate." In *Perspective: A New Freedom.* Vol. VII of the *ACTFL Review of Foreign Language Education.* Ed. Gilbert A. Jarvis and Alice C. Omaggio. Skokie, Ill.: National Textbook, 1975, pp. 47-92.

An extensive review of literature related to the concept of communicative competence.

Stevick, Earl W. *Memory, Meaning, and Method.* Rowley, Mass.: Newbury House, 1976.

In Chapter III the idea of cognitive depth in interaction is treated. Stevick takes issue with those who would limit the meaning of communication to the resolution of uncertainties.

Valette, Rebecca M. "Evaluating Oral and Written Communication: Suggestions for an Integrated Testing Program." *Language Learning,* 18 (1968), 111-120.

Presents rationale for developing criterion-referenced tests to measure oral and written communication.

**SPE
TECH**

INTRODUCTION

The articles in this section describe in detail specific techniques which can be used to promote real or at least realistic communication in the undeniably artificial setting of the foreign language classroom. To encourage comparison, we have loosely grouped the articles into categories. The first three articles, by Joiner, Omaggio and Gibson respectively, describe communicative activities built around games and puzzles. The small-group techniques outlined by Disick, by Birckbichler and and Bonin, and by Kalivoda, Elkins and Morain involve more ordinary and straightforward uses of language—interviewing, discussing, storytelling and the like.

The third category contains articles which describe strategies often associated with the humanistic education movement. Joiner and Zelson suggest simulation and role-playing activities for the foreign language classroom while Wolfe and Howe give examples in French and Spanish of a number of values clarification techniques which may be used to encourage communication on the affective level.

Diverse though they are, all the techniques have certain characteristics in common. They have been designed to motivate the student to communicate, to provide him with a need to talk or listen, a need to read or write. They attempt to engage the student personally—to capture his imagination, to arouse and sustain his interest. And perhaps most importantly, all the techniques involve the student in language use in the classroom which approximates language use in the real world outside.

Some of the techniques may be used immediately, lifted in their entirety from the articles; others may need to be modified or adapted to suit a particular situation or a particular textbook. Hopefully, all will serve as models or patterns for techniques of the teacher's own creation.

9

KEEP THEM GUESSING

Elizabeth G. Joiner
University of South Carolina

From *American Foreign Language Teacher,* Winter 1974.

Communication defined as the sending and receiving of messages is surely a major goal of the foreign language teacher. As evidence continues to accumulate that the pattern drills and exercises associated with the audiolingual approach have not necessarily produced adequate communicative ability, teachers and researchers alike have begun to investigate alternative modes of language practice—practice which is more personally meaningful to the student, more like the use he makes of his own native language. Palmer, for example, has created a technique for teaching specific structures through a type of communicative practice involving the creation of hypothetical situations and the selection of remarks appropriate to those circumstances;[1] and Rivers has suggested twelve natural uses of language which should serve to promote real communication in the foreign language classroom.[2]

While most foreign language teachers agree that they would like to help students communicate, many seem to feel that communication is not really possible in the earliest stages of language learning because of the limited vocabulary and structure available to the student. However, one technique which can be effective even with the beginning language learner is a kind of guessing game. This activity involves the students' imagination and sustains their interest. More importantly, it embodies a natural, normal use of language.

In order to make clear the contrast between real language and drill language, let us suppose that beginning students have learned to tell time. A drill activity might consist of the teacher's setting the hands of a clock at various times and asking "What time is it?" A variation of this would be to set the hands of the clock and say "Mary, it's six o'clock, isn't it?" While such drills provide the student an opportunity to practice using expressions of time, it is important to note that none of the times in the drill is really meaningful to the student because these times are in no way associated with events in the real world or even the classroom. Another important consideration is that the student has no freedom of choice regarding what he says; it is not he but the teacher who, by setting the hands of the clock, determines his reply.

A guessing game which would induce the students to repeat the same expressions of time under more realistic conditions might proceed as follows: The teacher using English instructs one student to think of the hour at which he went to bed last night. It will be the task of the other students to guess the time. This they do in the foreign language calling out "one a.m.," "eleven-thirty," "midnight," etc. When the correct time is guessed, it is written on the blackboard for visual reinforcement. To continue the game, another student is asked to think of the time he finished studying the previous night. When participating in such a guessing game, the student is technically free to say whatever he wishes; however, he must base his responses on what he knows about the real world—hours at which one usually goes to bed and the like.

Other guessing games which are particularly appropriate at the elementary level are grouped by topic and described below:

(1) Numbers. A student is told to think of a number between 1 and 50 or 50 and 100; the other students attempt to guess this number. Other guessing games involving numbers might include guessing the ages of other members of the class, the number of persons in the immediate families of other students, the number of beans in a glass jar, the number of games the football team will win or lose, etc.

(2) Dates. Students attempt to guess each other's birthdays. This may be divided into the month and day as there are obviously 365 possibilities. Once April has been identified as the birth month, however, the guesswork becomes easier. Limiting the number of questions to ten would force students to form them prudently. For example, instead of asking, "Is it May?, is it June?", etc., one would save questions by asking, "Is it between January and May?", etc. Another guessing game which would provide practice with dates consists of having one student to think of the date of an American or foreign holiday which the other students

must try to guess. Important dates in history might be used with students who are history buffs, but these should in some way be limited so that they will not be impossible to guess. The historic date might, for example, be limited to the French Revolution or the Spanish Civil War.

(3) Prices. Students are shown a number of objects and are asked to guess their price in the currency of the foreign country. To create a more realistic atmosphere, the prices can be printed on price tags which the teacher reveals as the price is guessed. In order to facilitate the guessing, upper and lower limits for each item may be given to the student. For variety, some articles which are sold by the liter or by kilogram could be included.

(4) Nouns. These are best restricted at least at first to certain logical groupings such as places, persons, foods, flowers, etc. To start the guessing, the teacher might bring a grocery bag to class and say, "I've been to the supermarket to buy food for dinner tonight. Who can guess what I bought?" As items are guessed they are removed from the bag so that students can see their hunches confirmed. A variation which involves only one individual at a time but which is always of great interest to the entire class consists of blindfolding one student and handing him objects to name aloud. Wax or plastic fruits and flowers, model cars and airplanes substitute nicely for the real thing in this activity. Still another intriguing guessing game involving nouns can be started by bringing to class a box or package the contents of which must be guessed by the students. They should be allowed to shake, squeeze and even smell the package if they wish.

(5) Verbs. Many verbs lend themselves readily to being "acted out." After the students have learned a number of verbs, the infinitives can be written on slips of paper to be drawn by individuals. Each must act out his verb so that the other members of the class can guess its meaning. If the class is very good at this, they may find pantomiming a conjugated verb form more challenging. In that case the pronoun and the verb must both be part of the charade. Another guessing game with verbs which would be appropriate at this level is the game known as *tipoter* in French. *Tipoter* is an artificial verb which can substitute for any regular -er verb. To begin the game, one student thinks of a verb. Then, the others must deduce what it is by asking questions such as "Can one *tipoter* in the church?" "Does one *tipoter* every day?" and the like. Artificial verbs like *tipoter* can be created for all the verb conjugations in French and, of course, for other languages as well.

Treats especially the idea that errors are evidence of learning strategies of second-language learners. Contains both practical and theoretical articles.

ulz, Renate A. "Discrete-Point versus Simulated Communication Testing in Foreign Languages." *Modern Language Journal,* 61 (1977), 94-101.

Distinguishes between the two types of tests and suggests that if communicative ability is the major aim of instruction, simulated communication tests tend to increase this kind of achievement.

ulz, Renate A., ed. *Teaching for Communication in the Foreign Language Classroom.* Skokie, Ill.: National Textbook, 1976.

Contains five articles specifically dealing with communication. Theory, classroom techniques and testing are included.

hulz, Renate A., and Walter H. Bartz. "Free to Communicate." In *Perspective: A New Freedom.* Vol. VII of the *ACTFL Review of Foreign Language Education.* Ed. Gilbert A. Jarvis and Alice C. Omaggio. Skokie, Ill.: National Textbook, 1975, pp. 47-92.

An extensive review of literature related to the concept of communicative competence.

evick, Earl W. *Memory, Meaning, and Method.* Rowley, Mass.: Newbury House, 1976.

In Chapter III the idea of cognitive depth in interaction is treated. Stevick takes issue with those who would limit the meaning of communication to the resolution of uncertainties.

alette, Rebecca M. "Evaluating Oral and Written Communication: Suggestions for an Integrated Testing Program." *Language Learning,* 18 (1968), 111-120.

Presents rationale for developing criterion-referenced tests to measure oral and written communication.

SPECIFIC
TECHNIQUES

INTRODUCTION

The articles in this section describe in detail specific techniques which can be used to promote real or at least realistic communication in the undeniably artificial setting of the foreign language classroom. To encourage comparison, we have loosely grouped the articles into categories. The first three articles, by Joiner, Omaggio and Gibson respectively, describe communicative activities built around games and puzzles. The small-group techniques outlined by Disick, by Birckbichler and and Bonin, and by Kalivoda, Elkins and Morain involve more ordinary and straightforward uses of language—interviewing, discussing, storytelling and the like.

The third category contains articles which describe strategies often associated with the humanistic education movement. Joiner and Zelson suggest simulation and role-playing activities for the foreign language classroom while Wolfe and Howe give examples in French and Spanish of a number of values clarification techniques which may be used to encourage communication on the affective level.

Diverse though they are, all the techniques have certain characteristics in common. They have been designed to motivate the student to communicate, to provide him with a need to talk or listen, a need to read or write. They attempt to engage the student personally—to capture his imagination, to arouse and sustain his interest. And perhaps most importantly, all the techniques involve the student in language use in the classroom which approximates language use in the real world outside.

Some of the techniques may be used immediately, lifted in their entirety from the articles; others may need to be modified or adapted to suit a particular situation or a particular textbook. Hopefully, all will serve as models or patterns for techniques of the teacher's own creation.

9

KEEP THEM GUESSING

Elizabeth G. Joiner
University of South Carolina

From *American Foreign Language Teacher,* Winter 1974.

Communication defined as the sending and receiving of messages is surely a major goal of the foreign language teacher. As evidence continues to accumulate that the pattern drills and exercises associated with the audiolingual approach have not necessarily produced adequate communicative ability, teachers and researchers alike have begun to investigate alternative modes of language practice—practice which is more personally meaningful to the student, more like the use he makes of his own native language. Palmer, for example, has created a technique for teaching specific structures through a type of communicative practice involving the creation of hypothetical situations and the selection of remarks appropriate to those circumstances;[1] and Rivers has suggested twelve natural uses of language which should serve to promote real communication in the foreign language classroom.[2]

While most foreign language teachers agree that they would like to help students communicate, many seem to feel that communication is not really possible in the earliest stages of language learning because of the limited vocabulary and structure available to the student. However, one technique which can be effective even with the beginning language learner is a kind of guessing game. This activity involves the students' imagination and sustains their interest. More importantly, it embodies a natural, normal use of language.

In order to make clear the contrast between real language and drill language, let us suppose that beginning students have learned to tell time. A drill activity might consist of the teacher's setting the hands of a clock at various times and asking "What time is it?" A variation of this would be to set the hands of the clock and say "Mary, it's six o'clock, isn't it?" While such drills provide the student an opportunity to practice using expressions of time, it is important to note that none of the times in the drill is really meaningful to the student because these times are in no way associated with events in the real world or even the classroom. Another important consideration is that the student has no freedom of choice regarding what he says; it is not he but the teacher who, by setting the hands of the clock, determines his reply.

A guessing game which would induce the students to repeat the same expressions of time under more realistic conditions might proceed as follows: The teacher using English instructs one student to think of the hour at which he went to bed last night. It will be the task of the other students to guess the time. This they do in the foreign language calling out "one a.m.," "eleven-thirty," "midnight," etc. When the correct time is guessed, it is written on the blackboard for visual reinforcement. To continue the game, another student is asked to think of the time he finished studying the previous night. When participating in such a guessing game, the student is technically free to say whatever he wishes; however, he must base his responses on what he knows about the real world—hours at which one usually goes to bed and the like.

Other guessing games which are particularly appropriate at the elementary level are grouped by topic and described below:

(1) Numbers. A student is told to think of a number between 1 and 50 or 50 and 100; the other students attempt to guess this number. Other guessing games involving numbers might include guessing the ages of other members of the class, the number of persons in the immediate families of other students, the number of beans in a glass jar, the number of games the football team will win or lose, etc.

(2) Dates. Students attempt to guess each other's birthdays. This may be divided into the month and day as there are obviously 365 possibilities. Once April has been identified as the birth month, however, the guesswork becomes easier. Limiting the number of questions to ten would force students to form them prudently. For example, instead of asking, "Is it May?, is it June?", etc., one would save questions by asking, "Is it between January and May?", etc. Another guessing game which would provide practice with dates consists of having one student to think of the date of an American or foreign holiday which the other students

must try to guess. Important dates in history might be used with students who are history buffs, but these should in some way be limited so that they will not be impossible to guess. The historic date might, for example, be limited to the French Revolution or the Spanish Civil War.

(3) Prices. Students are shown a number of objects and are asked to guess their price in the currency of the foreign country. To create a more realistic atmosphere, the prices can be printed on price tags which the teacher reveals as the price is guessed. In order to facilitate the guessing, upper and lower limits for each item may be given to the student. For variety, some articles which are sold by the liter or by kilogram could be included.

(4) Nouns. These are best restricted at least at first to certain logical groupings such as places, persons, foods, flowers, etc. To start the guessing, the teacher might bring a grocery bag to class and say, "I've been to the supermarket to buy food for dinner tonight. Who can guess what I bought?" As items are guessed they are removed from the bag so that students can see their hunches confirmed. A variation which involves only one individual at a time but which is always of great interest to the entire class consists of blindfolding one student and handing him objects to name aloud. Wax or plastic fruits and flowers, model cars and airplanes substitute nicely for the real thing in this activity. Still another intriguing guessing game involving nouns can be started by bringing to class a box or package the contents of which must be guessed by the students. They should be allowed to shake, squeeze and even smell the package if they wish.

(5) Verbs. Many verbs lend themselves readily to being "acted out." After the students have learned a number of verbs, the infinitives can be written on slips of paper to be drawn by individuals. Each must act out his verb so that the other members of the class can guess its meaning. If the class is very good at this, they may find pantomiming a conjugated verb form more challenging. In that case the pronoun and the verb must both be part of the charade. Another guessing game with verbs which would be appropriate at this level is the game known as *tipoter* in French. *Tipoter* is an artificial verb which can substitute for any regular -er verb. To begin the game, one student thinks of a verb. Then, the others must deduce what it is by asking questions such as "Can one *tipoter* in the church?" "Does one *tipoter* every day?" and the like. Artificial verbs like *tipoter* can be created for all the verb conjugations in French and, of course, for other languages as well.

(6) Colors and other adjectives. Almost every student has a favorite actor, actress or singer whom he can describe in detail. The teacher, then, might ask one student to think of her favorite male singer. The rest of the class would be instructed to guess the singer's identity through asking questions about his physical appearance such as "Is he tall?" "Does he have blue eyes?" "Does he have long blond hair?" etc. This activity may be varied by sending one student into the hall while the other class members decide on a "mystery person"—a politician, an entertainer, or even one of the members of the class. When he returns from the hallway, the student must try to guess the identity of the person by asking questions about his or her physical appearance.

The guessing games previously described give the beginning student practice in speaking the foreign language at least to a limited extent. Such games may also be used quite effectively for listening practice at the elementary level. The teacher might, for example, say to the class: "Today I went to a small shop near my apartment. It smelled very good and was quite warm inside. Behind the counter was a very pleasant woman from whom I bought a loaf of bread and some breakfast rolls. Where did I go?" Students may be encouraged to raise their hands as soon as they think they know the answer as some will surely put together the clues more rapidly than others. For another listening game, the teacher could say: "I'm thinking of a small animal with a long tail. He has small ears and either long or short fur. His favorite places seem to be near a warm stove or in a window. His favorite food is milk. What is this animal?" The important concern here, of course, is not that the students recognize that cats have long tails and short ears but that they be able to use their listening ability in order to make an intelligent guess.

While the above suggestions for guessing games cover several areas generally included in a beginning language course, the list is by no means exhaustive. The creative teacher will be able to add to his repertoire by inventing games pertaining specifically to his own language goals and materials. Quiz shows on television and parlor games such as charades and Botticelli can provide valuable models for games for more advanced students.

Because everyone loves a mystery, guessing games have built-in motivation, and they can be made even more exciting by dividing the class into teams and competing for small prizes. It should be noted, however, that even "fun" things can be overdone. While they offer a lively means of providing the beginning student with real language practice, guessing games should not be the only communicative activity of the class. Used judiciously and in combination with other kinds of real language practice, however, guessing games can contribute to the development of communicative competency even in the early stages of language learning. Remember that this type of activity is more than just fun and games—it is real language use.

NOTES

1. Palmer, Adrian, "Teaching Communication," *Language Learning,* Vol. 20, No. 1, June 1970, pp. 55-68.

2. Rivers, Wilga. *Speaking in Many Tongues,* Newbury House, Rowley, Mass., 1976, pp. 31-33.

REAL COMMUNICATION:

SPEAKING A LIVING LANGUAGE

Alice Omaggio
ERIC Clearinghouse on Language and Linguistics

From *Foreign Language Annals,* vol. 9, no. 2 (April 1976), pp. 131-133.

> *All speech is a dead language, until it finds a willing listener.*
> Robert Louis Stevenson

For most foreign language teachers the term "dead language" would probably bring to mind piles of dusty scrolls of ancient and forgotten dialects or, more simply, those languages such as Latin or Classical Greek that are no longer commonly spoken. The term "living language," by contrast, would be descriptive of the French, Spanish, or other modern language they teach. Ironically, to too many foreign language students the term "dead language" seems to characterize very accurately their day-to-day experiences in the modern language classroom, especially if their verbal activity consists largely of mechanistic, manipulative, artificially contrived conversations devised for oral practice and imposed upon them. We too often overlook the fact that communication is a function of *need.* If we hope to achieve genuine communication in our classrooms—if we want our students to speak a living language—we must create the need to talk and the need to listen. The students must truly want to hear each other, or they might as well be conversing with a tape recorder.

To encourage our students to converse with each other we can adapt a human relations technique described in the February 1975 issue of *Psychology Today* in an article entitled "The Jigsaw Route to Learning and Liking." The "Jigsaw Puzzle Method" was designed to promote better relations among the races in integrated schools by creating two needs within the students: (1) to communicate with one another, and (2) to serve as resources for each other in problem-solving activities. Basically, the technique works on the principle of the jigsaw puzzle: each student in a group has a piece of information, but only by combining pieces can the group members put the puzzle together. Cooperation, careful listening, and understanding are essential if the puzzle pieces are to form a complete picture.

The technique is easily adaptable to foreign language classrooms, and it provides a conceptual tool for creating new activities, modifying old ones, or seeing classroom behavior in a new light. A few examples of small-group activities using the jigsaw puzzle method follow.

1. GAMES

Each student in a small group is given a picture of an object that he must describe to the others *without* using the name of the object directly. The first letter of the name of each object is then recorded, and the combined letters spell out a group word. For example, French students may be given the following objects to describe:

Student 1: cahier
Student 2: robe
Student 3: argent
Student 4: immeuble
Student 5: école

The group word formed from the first letter of each object would be *craie,* and the puzzle would be complete.

A variation of this game involves puzzle parts depicting objects that are part of a scene to be guessed, such as pieces of furniture in a room. Groups within the class might be in competition for the first completion of the puzzle.

Another variation would be the use of descriptive phrases or sentences (perhaps on cards) as the puzzle parts. All the statements, when combined, provide an adequate description of an object that the group must then identify. Cards with more specific descriptors could be provided if the object is not guessed on the first round.

Puzzle parts might also describe a personality—perhaps a character from a television show, a political figure, or an individual in the school (a teacher, staff member, or student that the members of the group would know). The game could proceed in the manner of Twenty Questions; however, no one member of the group knows who the personality is. Each student holds a card containing one piece of descriptive information (physical traits, nationality, occupation, etc.) that the others in the group must elicit from him through questioning. When all the available information has been conveyed and pieced together, group members make a collective guess as to the identity of the mystery personality. The group that makes the correct identification first would win the game.

Student-Generated Material
The above activity could be modified by asking each student in the class to write a description of himself on 3 x 5 cards—perhaps four or five separate cards could be used to provide information about his interests, his physical appearance, his family, or any other facts about himself that he would like to convey to others in the class. (Because the student provides the information about himself, there is no danger of hurt feelings.) Each student has thus created a personal jigsaw puzzle to be used by the small groups in the class.

Multiple Puzzles
A more complicated version of these activities might involve multiple puzzles to be solved. For a group of five, for example, several *sets* of cards could be made: each set of five cards depicts four objects that go together conceptually—four cards depicting food, four cards depicting clothing, etc.—and one "odd" card. The group members describe to each other the objects represented on their cards (being careful not to let the others see the card). For each set of five cards, the group decides which object does not belong with the others and sets it aside. When several sets of cards have thus been described and sorted, the group takes all of the odd cards and tries to determine what concept they represent. All of the odd cards might depict the rooms of a house, modes of transportation, or types of animals. When the concept has been correctly identified, the puzzle is complete.

2. NARRATIVE CONSTRUCTION

Each student in a group of four or five individuals is given a part of a story, anecdote, or other narrative material. Each one tells his part of the story in turn (the parts could be numbered sequentially), and all members of the group are responsible for the entire content of the narrative that they have constructed together by means of mutual, active listening and speaking.

An interesting variation might be the use of cartoons that tell a story. The *Peanuts* cartoons, for example, have been translated into several modern languages, as well as Latin, and could be conveniently used in this activity. Each member of the group receives one frame of the cartoon sequence. He must describe the action that is taking place in as much detail as possible, conveying any dialogue that appears in his frame as well. The group then pieces the frames together in their proper sequence; for a follow-up activity students might write a résumé of the narrative, including as many details as they can remember from their group discussion.

3. CULTURE CAPSULES

Rather than relying on a culture capsule presentation by the teacher, students can share the responsibility of teaching one another various facts about a given cultural concept. For example, in discussing French bread, each student could be responsible for transmitting a piece of information that would normally be included in a culture capsule:

Student 1: The importance of bread to the French family; bread as a national symbol.

Student 2: A description of the French *baguette*.

Student 3: The way in which bread is eaten at the table in France.

Student 4: Proverbs and sayings that depict bread and its importance to French life.

The group could then summarize together the ways in which French and American bread differ, basing their conclusions upon the information that they provided each other.

4. PROVERBS AND CLICHÉS

A list of proverbs (or clichés) in the foreign language could be provided to members of the group, along with a short narrative that has been divided into parts. The narrative describes a situation that is illustrative of one of the sayings. For example, a story could be constructed illustrating the problem, "A stitch in time saves nine." Each student receives a part of the story and is responsible for conveying that information to the others in the group. The puzzle is complete when the group discovers the proverb from the list that applies to their particular situation.

The possible applications of this technique are as abundant as are its benefits in promoting student-centered learning and real communication in the language. Not only do students feel a genuine *need to speak and listen to each other,* but also every individual perceives his contribution to the group effort as important and worthwhile. If the results of the Jigsaw Puzzle Method obtained in the integrated schools, as described in *Psychology Today,* are replicated in our classrooms, students will develop respect for each other's needs and will leave the experience with more confidence in themselves and in their ability to communicate in the foreign language.

THE STRIP STORY:
A CATALYST FOR COMMUNICATION

Robert E. Gibson
University of Hawaii

From *TESOL Quarterly,* June 1975. Copyright 1975 by the Teachers of English to Speakers of Other Languages. Reprinted by permission of the publisher and Robert E. Gibson.

Teachers of English as a second language, especially those who teach adults, have been plagued by a great number of obstacles in their attempts to create real, not just realistic,[1] communicative learning situations in their classrooms. Many have struggled endlessly with dialogues, attempting to write more realistic ones and then trying to make them come alive in their classrooms. For such teachers, attempting to create realistic structure drills has probably been even more of a problem since the very nature of the technique, tight control, tends to stifle anything resembling functional use of language, namely communication. Many ESL teachers have attempted to use something like "free conversation" sessions to encourage real communication only to have such sessions degenerate into dull exchanges revolving around what William Labov has termed "known answer" questions.

One example of a "known answer" question is John asking Marcia where she came from when he knows full well where she came from and she knows he knows (Labov 1970). Although such exchanges resemble functional uses of language, they are far from it since the primary function of language is to communicate unpredictable information.

These sessions are typically all too predictable. If it is assumed that the primary goal of language classes is to help students to develop communicative abilities, it is easy to see why the techniques that I have mentioned rarely accomplish that goal. They rarely approach real communication and they either exert too much control over the communicative exercise or not enough. Too much control stifles and not enough overwhelms.

Almost by accident, I discovered a technique that appears to overcome many of the difficulties in creating real communication lessons while at the same time retaining control over those aspects of the linguistic signals or content that are appropriate. The·technique appears at first glance to be nothing more than a scrambled sentence exercise used by almost everyone at one time or another. However there are a few critical differences—differences that provide the spark which makes language classes come alive. For a reason that will become obvious, I call it the "Strip Story."

In preparation for the lesson, the teacher selects a story or anecdote which has the same number of sentences as there are students. Simple sentences can be combined or more complex ones broken up to make the appropriate number of sentences. The sentences are typed and dittoed with extra space between each sentence. One copy is cut into strips, with one sentence on each strip. In class the sentences are distributed at random to the students, who are then asked to memorize their sentences. No more than a minute is allowed for memorization. Students are not allowed to write anything down or to compare sentences at this time. After the sentences are memorized, the strips are thrown away, the story remaining only in the students' heads. The idea is to have each student become the sole source of one piece of information. Being the only source of his sentence will force the student to speak at least once. Thus everyone is required to participate in order to solve the problem. Next the students are instructed to find out exactly what the story is without writing anything down. Then the teacher sits down and remains silent. This part of the procedure is crucial because if it is not followed, the students will rely on the teacher to do the thinking and speaking. It is probably the most difficult thing in the world for the teacher to do what is necessary here, *nothing*.

The first time a class does a Strip Story, there are several uncomfortable minutes of silence, coupled with meaningful glances in the direction of the teacher—who in turn ignores them, except possibly to encourage the students to get up out of their chairs and talk to each other, much as they would at a cocktail party. After this the teacher should really be quiet, listening and observing.

Just how the students go about reconstructing the story varies from class to class. Sometimes a natural leader will emerge, asking questions, suggesting ways of going about it. Other times, each student begins by talking to one other student, gradually including more people until the whole class is involved. Invariably, however, at some time the group will hear all the sentences, typically many times. After the sentences are heard a few times, the organization of all this disconnected information takes place. With this technique, it is not possible to predict many of the outcomes, or all of the points that will be learned. One thing is certain, however; students teach themselves and each other, faster and more effectively, many of the things that teachers ordinarily have great difficulty teaching. I will say more about this point later.

After a period of time in which all the sentences are organized (and this is normally done by physical positioning of students), the group usually agrees on a given sequence. When they are satisfied, the teacher rejoins the group and asks them to repeat the story in sequence, each person saying his part. It does not matter so much whether the students get the proper sequence or not at this stage.

Next, follow-up activities can be done. Individual students can be asked to repeat the entire story at this time with help when needed from the group. Tenses can be changed, pronouns reversed, or other parts of the story manipulated at this time also. Next it is useful to ask the students to write the entire story down, taking dictation from each other. This forces accuracy in pronunciation and listening and also provides them with copies of the story to use in subsequent activities. After everything has been done with the story, the original is then passed out for comparison. If the original varies from their versions, all kinds of discussions about the differences emerge naturally, spontaneously. Often these discussions go on long after class, in the halls and in the dormitories.

It might appear that solving the problem of putting the story back together is the most important part of the procedure. It is not. What happens as a result of the students' attempts to solve the problem is the real meat of this technique.

First of all, students must all participate actively, contributing information, asking questions. The speech events are truly communication, since people are getting and giving unpredictable information as in real communication. The complexity of such language usually increases when the focus is taken off the language and put on some external subject, in this case the story problem. Students also find it essential, often for the first time, to listen to each other instead of the teacher. This is one major reason for the teacher to stay out of the process. The communication during this technique is highly diverse; questions, answers, statements, arguments, summaries, and definitions all are used naturally by the students. The talk is fast and furious with very few dead spots. Even though it takes a while to get started, it happens.

A note about the importance of memorizing the sentences is in order. By forcing the students to store all the information in their heads, the stage is set for instances of real communication. One person who allowed his class to keep the strips had some extremely quiet students that day. Since his students could take the sentences around and fit them together physically, there was no need to talk, and they did not. Like electricity, they took the path of least resistance. The problem was solved in a matter of minutes and that was that.

The choice of content does not seem to be an important factor in getting the students to interact with each other and to work actively toward the solution of the problem. Stories have been used that range from Aesop's Fables to the sinking of the Titanic to a simple sequence of a bed catching fire due to a careless smoker. Regardless of how simple, childish, or inconsequential the content might appear to be, it results in great enthusiasm and interest. Of course the content can be designed with several purposes in mind. If pronoun reference problems are appropriate material for a given class, such problems can be built into the story. One good thing about this technique is that the generalizations, such as those referring to pronoun use, emerge naturally as a result of trying to get the story back together correctly.

One exchange that was observed by an instructor when he used this technique concerned the use of *they* prior to any specific reference of who *they* was. The students had tentatively put the story together with a sentence beginning with *they*. After feeling uncomfortable with this arrangement for a while, one student finally asked, "Who is *they*?" A long discussion followed about whom this *they* referred to. However, the final statement made by one of the students was to the effect that you need to specify the noun before you can refer to it using a personal pronoun. Most teachers who have tried to teach this item will agree that it is almost never easy. In this case the students taught themselves in a way that was completely meaningful. This kind of discussion resulting in various generalizations of language and stylistic rules arises naturally when this technique is used. The strength of rules like these is that they have a direct bearing on students' active communication. Students actually experience non-communication until they make these adjustments. Then rules have functional value: that is, they actually further communication.

Besides learning grammatical points from each other, students often make radical improvement in their pronunciation during a single period. The crux of the Strip Story problem is understanding and being understood. Often an individual student's pronunciation is poor, but the student feels it is not a serious problem. Under such circumstances, most adult students will make little progress in pronunciation. It is easy for them to attribute their pronunciation problems to an over-critical teacher. However, when the Strip Story is used, every student must be understood or the technique will not work. After trying several times to say something, each time being met by quizzical stares or by "What?" or by "Would you repeat please?" students become convinced that they do have a serious problem, serious because it prevents them from being understood. Until that realization is reached, I am convinced that most adults will make no significant progress in pronunciation.

One example of radical pronunciation improvement happened with a Japanese speaker who had a great difficulty with the American English postvocalic /r/ and with consonant clusters. In that story this student had the only sentence with the phrase *saber-toothed-tiger* in it, which was necessary for the solution to the story. After the student tried many times to make herself understood, to no avail, another student asked her to spell it. She did. The other student said, "Oh, you mean saber-toothed tiger" whereupon the Japanese student repeated the phrase perfectly. I could have drilled her for six months on her pronunciation difficulties in this phrase without achieving that result. She finally realized that her pronunciation prevented her from being understood and only then did she correct it. I suspect that the greatest barrier to adults learning better pronunciation is that they are not in the least convinced that it constitutes a real communication problem. Only after they believe they have a problem can they solve it.

Every time this technique is used, some unpredictable learning takes place as a result. For this reason, the teacher's role as an observer becomes very useful. By not directing the procedure, the teacher is free to take notes on problems and to acknowledge problems that are being dealt with effectively. The Strip Story allows the teacher to combine control (content, length and complexity of the actual sentences) with freedom (students interacting with each other in dealing with the sentences). Thus the teacher can have the cake and eat it too.

There are several other positive things that are noticeable about a class when this technique is used. The teacher's role becomes one of a facilitator of learning, a role to which much lip service, but little more, has been paid. Such a role is often uncomfortable since the teacher appears to be doing nothing. Imagine just sitting there watching students learn. When this technique is used, the environment is much freer and non-threatening. Students also notice, many for the first time, that they can and do learn from each other. The teacher also discovers that vocabulary items need no explanation because someone in the class often will already know the word in question. One person is enough. If the student who has the word can spell it, someone in the group can provide the meaning. Active participation by all of the students in each other's learning is the key to the success of this procedure.

To conclude, the Strip Story began as an attempt to teach something about sequence, but turned out to be something quite different and more important. It turned out to be the most effective way I have used to get students to communicate with each other while simultaneously providing a springboard from which all sorts of usually difficult items are learned painlessly and quickly. The technique allows the teacher a certain amount of control, but does not stifle attempts at real communication. Since I first used the procedure, several other teachers have also used it with widely varying groups—high and basic levels, adults and children, university and adult education students—all with a high degree of success. Each time it is used, it opens up further possibilities for providing interesting, effective, and enjoyable ESL classes, all based on the functional use of the language.

NOTE

1. For an expansion of this distinction see Stevick (1971, 29-31).

REFERENCES

Labov, William. 1970. Finding out what children can do with language. *Working Papers in Communication.* Pacific Speech Association, *1,* 1, 1-30. P. 10 talks about "known answer" questions.

Stevick, Earl. 1971. *Adapting and writing language lessons.* Washington, D.C. Foreign Service Institute.

12

DEVELOPING COMMUNICATION SKILLS
THROUGH SMALL GROUP TECHNIQUES

Renée S. Disick
Valley Stream Central High School, New York

From *American Foreign Language Teacher,* Winter 1972.

Ideas on teaching foreign languages have been evolving these past few years. There has been a movement away from pure stimulus-response techniques toward greater emphasis on student creativity and the generation of new utterances. Teachers have become increasingly aware of the abyss separating a student's ability to perform a pattern drill and his ability to communicate original ideas. In addition, student desires for relevance in what they are taught as well as more active involvement in the learning process call for a rethinking of the activities which go on in the classroom. The purpose, then, of this article is to explore possible contributions which small-group activities might make toward the development of student ability to communicate orally and in writing.

As used here, "ability to communicate" excludes certain common classroom activities. It is not choral repetition or written copying; it is not spoken or written pattern drills or sentence transformations; it is not well-rehearsed answers to familiar questions. Though these activities do provide students with necessary foundation skills, free communication entails something more. It involves creating new sentences to express one's own ideas. If students are to develop communication ability, they need practice in unguided, free-answer situations. Lots of practice. Much more than can be provided in teacher-centered classrooms where only one person talks at a time.

Additional practice-time can be offered by restructuring student-teacher relationships in the classroom. One part of the lesson can be devoted to the teacher's presentation to the full class and the other part to related small-group activities such as the following ones:

1. *Purpose*: To develop grammatical accuracy and increase oral participation in drillwork.

Procedure: The teacher presents the new grammar and pattern drills. Students break into pairs to practice the material with each taking a turn cueing and responding. If answers are not provided in the book, then dittoed response sheets can be distributed.

Comments: As opposed to what occurs during full-class drills, students working in pairs do not mouth rather than vocalize their responses, nor do they tune out the activity. By breaking the monotony of choral response and increasing student involvement, this technique often reduces the time needed for drills and improves student performance on them. (Though this activity does not strictly involve free communication, it is useful for developing pronunciation ease in Level I and II students.)

2. *Purpose*: To develop ability to comprehend and use orally the new vocabulary and structure of the lesson.

Procedure: The teacher distributes a sheet of dittoed conversation questions based on the new words and new grammar of the current unit. If necessary, these may be practiced with the entire class before group work begins. Semi-complete model answers may also be distributed and the class divided into pairs. One person asks a question and checks his partner's responses against the answer key. Afterwards, roles are reversed. Students in Levels I and II can do this.

Comments: The teacher may announce a follow-up assignment of an oral or written quiz over the material.

3. *Purpose*: To develop ability to ask and answer questions.

Procedure: Each student prepares three to five questions about families, friends, likes and dislikes, leisure activities, etc. Student questions are compiled into a questionnaire and "interviewers" or "census-takers" poll students in groups of four or five. Student responses may be recorded and tabulated with the results announced to the class.

Comments: The assignment might be expanded by having students write compositions on to what extent their personal answers do or do not conform to those of the majority of the class. This is an effective way of reviewing comparatives and of capitalizing on natural student interest in themselves and in their friends. The activity is suitable at Levels I and II.

4. *Purpose*: To develop listening, speaking, and reading ability.

Procedure: The class is assigned a reading text to be discussed the next day in groups of four. The teacher hands out a list of detail-type questions to strong students appointed to lead the groups. The leaders ask the questions, and the members look for the answers in the text. When a person answers, however, he must do so without looking in the book. Whenever possible, he should be encouraged to use his own words. This works at Levels I and II.

Comments: This activity eliminates the need for spot quizzes in order to find out whether or not students have done their reading homework. Students generally tend to prepare their assignments so they can participate in the activity. Even if a student has not read the material at home, the teacher can at least be reasonably sure that he will read it in class. A worthwhile follow-up to this activity is a reading or vocabulary test on what was discussed.

5. *Purpose*: To develop ability to speak or write fluently.

Procedure: The class is shown a magazine picture for which they must make up an appropriate story. Groups of four or five try to agree on a plausible story which is either written down by a "secretary" or communicated orally by a "reporter." Different interpretations from each group may be presented to the full class as a listening comprehension activity.

Comments: An alternative assignment would be to read an incomplete story to the class and have different groups invent conclusions for it. Or, they could create imaginative continuations of stories they have finished reading. Allowing for different degrees of sophistication, students in Levels I through III may carry out the activity.

6. *Purpose*: To develop ability to speak fluently in more or less impromptu situations.

Procedure: The teacher or students write out ideas for skits on 3" x 5" index cards. Groups of two or three students draw a card, choose roles, prepare their thoughts, then act out the situation. The skits may or may not be presented to the full class. Once the conversation possibilities on the first card have been exhausted, students draw a new one from the pack.

Comments: Stimulating situations for skits involve *conflicts*—between siblings, between parents and children, between students and teachers. Ideas can also be based on material in current or review textbook lessons. This activity is most effective with advanced Level II, Level III or IV students.

7. *Purpose*: To develop ability to write creatively and with grammatical accuracy.

Procedure: Students work in groups of not more than three writing a composition on a given topic. Using dictionaries and grammar books, they help each other write correctly and, when needed, ask for the teacher's help in expressing their ideas.

Comments: The teacher may suggest one or several topics or may list five to ten unrelated words to be incorporated into a coherent narrative or dialogue. Another possibility is to have students demonstrate their ability to use correctly five or more examples of the grammar currently under study. Assigning a group grade is possible, or the composition could be written just for practice. Both Level I and II students can profit from this activity which can be an effective transitional step toward individually written work.

8. *Purpose*: To develop ability to speak freely on a given topic.

Procedure: The class is given a controversial discussion topic and forms groups of four to six. They choose a leader who tries to lead the members toward a consensus. At the end of the allotted time, each leader summarizes for the class the discussion his group has had.

Comments: The discussion topic can be announced in advance or immediately before the discussion period. It may relate to politics, social problems, or academic issues. A variation of this might be to culminate an art unit by having groups of students discuss their reactions to an unfamiliar painting by an artist they have studied. Level IV students should be able to handle this activity successfully.

The activities just described are those which have worked in the author's classes. The list, however, is far from exhaustive. It is hoped that the ideas mentioned may stimulate the reader to think of others applying to the specific needs of his own particular teaching situation. The effort is worthwhile because small-group activities offer several advantages.

Conversation in a small group of friends helps to reduce the tension learners feel when asked to speak a strange language. Talking in front of the teacher and the whole class can be somewhat frightening for many students and can inhibit their use of new, untried responses. In small groups, however, student fears of being wrong, of being laughed at, of displaying ignorance or inadequacies are significantly reduced. Conversing with classmates of equal language competence—or incompetence—is far less intimidating than conversing with a seemingly omnipotent bilingual teacher who apparently never makes mistakes.

Another advantage inherent in small group work is that it increases student attention and involvement. A normal teacher engaging in normal classroom activities simply cannot succeed every day in holding the undivided attention of each of thirty different individuals seated before him. (Exceptions to this statement include: specially prepared audio-visual material, guest lecturers, and teacher headstands and cartwheels.) Problems of maintaining attention day in and day out are considerably alleviated when students are involved in small-group activities.

Lack of student participation in class discussions is another problem which small-group work can help solve. Seen from a student's point of view, constantly volunteering to answer questions can be quite ridiculous. Assuming that a teacher tries to provide equal speaking opportunities to all thirty of his students, then each one can answer probably no more than once or twice per session. Once a student has produced the requisite number of responses, he may be reasonably sure of not having to answer again that day (unless the teacher tries to "get him" for not paying attention). Thus, it is pointless to continue raising one's hand unless one enjoys the exercise or wishes to impress the teacher. Such a situation cannot exist in small conversation groups.

There may also be some negative aspects to small-group activities, like student discipline and classroom noise level. Actually, though, these need not pose major problems. Student behavior in a properly structured and supervised group is usually no worse—and often much better—than in a conventional teacher vs. class relationship. Nor does the sound of several people talking at once pose a serious obstacle. When properly controlled, the simultaneous responses of even ten students produce only a general background noise which does not interfere significantly with communication.

The strongest criticism of group work has to do with accuracy of student responses. Don't many errors made in class go uncorrected? Don't students establish bad language habits when speaking among themselves? How can students learn accurate pronunciation and correct speech patterns unless the teacher corrects what they say?

In response, it should be noted that if students make fewer uncorrected mistakes in a teacher-centered class, this is because they make fewer responses and have less chance to err. Nothing ventured, nothing lost—or gained either, for that matter. It is also important to consider that speaking ability consists of two major elements: fluency as well as grammatical accuracy. Strict insistence on grammatical correctness at all times tends to inhibit student responses and prevents the development of fluency. Correct forms are obviously required for educated, intelligible speech; however, when speaking ability is in the process of development, correctness should be sacrificed *at times* in order to develop ease, fluency, and confidence. If teacher concern for accuracy is nevertheless strong, then each student can be required to pass an oral check before being allowed to continue on to new material.

Above all else, though, beginning and intermediate students need to feel the satisfaction of being able to use the foreign language to communicate their own ideas. They need to be convinced that language study has a real purpose, that it is much more than a series of sterile exercises. Delaying communication until students have sufficient command of the language is to deny them a prime reward of their learning and to discourage them from further study. It is also preferable to develop in students habits of self-correction rather than fostering their reliance on teacher-correction. Students need to free themselves from dependence on a teacher and must learn to assume responsibility for their own continued foreign language progress.

Two essential elements of successful communication in small groups are structure and supervision. An assignment must be communicated clearly so that each student is sure of what he is expected to do. The difference between mass chaos and fruitful learning depends in part on students' knowing where to sit, with whom, what material they need, what they are to do, and how much time they have in which to do it. Groups may be allowed to form freely or they may be initially teacher-designated. Trusting students to form their own groups normally works quite well; students choose friends they like and with whom they can work comfortably. Without teacher direction, the groups usually turn out fairly homogeneous. After a teacher has acquainted himself with his students, the direction or manipulation of group membership can be minimal, since well-functioning groups tend to remain together.

Once the necessary instructions are given, the teacher can visit each group to be sure students understand what to do and are doing it. Since small-group work is considerably more relaxed than a teacher-dominated situation, some irrelevant conversations among students can be expected. It is debatable, however, whether its net effect on learning is more detrimental than the daydreaming, clock-watching, and note-passing which may go on in a traditionally run classroom.

When the groups are well under way the teacher can walk around spending some time with each. Corrections can be made, if necessary, or students can ask questions on what they do not understand. Students in groups are considerably more eager to ask for explanations than they are in the full class. Not only do they feel less "stupid" about not understanding the material when surrounded only by a few friends, but they consider the teacher to be more accessible to them and more willing to help with individual problems. Though the teacher may want to praise student work, if merited, this is not a primary goal of group activities. Teacher praise and encouragement has been greatly—if not overly—emphasized in language teaching; yet, it is equally if not more important that students become critical of themselves and learn to improve the quality of their work independently of the teacher's judgment. In some cases, the teacher might choose to lead the slowest group in order to offer the compensatory instruction needed to overcome learning difficulties. If so, then more advanced students who volunteer to serve as aides during their free periods can provide help to other students.

The new relationships which emerge in small-group work deserve to be noted. The relationship of teacher vs. class, a confrontation of adversaries more worthy of courtroom than classroom, is eliminated. The game of winning teacher approval and higher grades by constantly raising one's hand—and denying speaking opportunities to others—can no longer be played. Rather than serving as an opponent to be pleased, outwitted, or manipulated, the teacher becomes a source of help and information for those who need it. Instead of competing frantically for grades and favor, students learn to help each other with classwork. Students feel less reserved about asking questions of student aides or classmates, than of a sometimes intimidating adult. This relationship of learning from peers can—and often does—continue outside the classroom. In this way students come to realize that acquiring knowledge need not be confined to one place, or one time, or one person. Learning is something which can go on throughout one's life—even after leaving school, diploma in hand.

Though there is much to recommend the use of small-group work it is by no means a utopian solution to all the difficulties of teaching foreign languages. Problems may result because two or more students are either too friendly or too hostile. These disturbances may be minimized if the teacher is sensitive at all times to the dynamics of group interaction and makes necessary changes tactfully, but firmly. More serious difficulties can arise from the fact that groups often vary considerably in the amount of time they legitimately need to complete an assignment. If a group finishes early, assigning more of the same work is inadvisable, since in effect this penalizes diligence. Instead, these students could be allowed to read foreign language books or magazines available in class for this purpose. They might also spend the extra time on individual projects. Or, if the end of the period is near, a few relaxed minutes of doing nothing can be their reward.

To a teacher accustomed to "keeping together" a class of thirty, the considerable variations in work-time displayed when students are allowed to learn at their own pace may come as quite a shock. These widely divergent workrates point up rather dramatically the need to provide for the wide range in ability of students who are nevertheless placed in one "homogeneously-grouped" class. In such cases, the teacher may decide to go all the way—to switch completely to an open-classroom, continuous progress system in which explanations are offered when needed and students take tests when ready.

So far, the advantages group work offers to students have been stressed. But teachers can also benefit from using this technique. Group work relieves the strain of having to maintain for long periods of time both the attention and good behavior of twenty-five to thirty different individuals. It eases the pressure of constantly being onstage presenting new material and repeating explanations some student may be too bored to hear. It permits teachers to work *with* students, rather than against them, as demanding—though well-meaning—critics. It frees a teacher's attention from pre-occupation with his own words and actions, and allows him to see, feel, and understand the needs of his student. This awareness and sensitivity to learners is what transforms teaching from a science into an art.

It has been suggested that small-group work can be incorporated profitably into the repertoire of language teaching techniques. Its successful application can offer the joy of communication, not only to students, but to their teachers as well.

REAL COMMUNICATION
THROUGH INTERVIEW
AND CONVERSATION CARDS

Thérèse M. Bonin *and* Diane W. Birckbichler
Ohio State University

From *The Modern Language Journal,* January/February 1975.

Communicative competence is being increasingly emphasized as one of the major objectives of foreign language study. Teaching strategies are no longer viewed from a narrow standpoint of methodological orthodoxy or in terms of allegiance to a single teaching method, but rather from a viewpoint of their effectiveness in furthering true ability to communicate in the foreign language. At the same time, there is a growing awareness and a new concern for the student as an individual—a concern for his personal interests, his goals, and his learning characteristics. It is not at all surprising that these two emphases should have surfaced at the same time, for they both focus upon the student: on the one hand, upon his behavior and on the other, what he brings to the teaching/learning situation. It is these same emphases that validate and justify the "conversation and interview cards" described in this article.

RATIONALE

If students are to communicate in the foreign language, we must recognize that they are more likely to want to communicate about something that concerns them in a very personal way. A large amount of all daily communication between individuals involves wanting to know about the other person—what he did, what he thought—as well as wanting to reveal oneself to that other person.

The purpose of the proposed procedures is to try to capitalize on these interests. To the degree that facets of the student's personality and experience are what he most keenly wants to communicate (and conversely, what is of greatest interest to other students), the proposed procedures will enhance language learning. It has further been established that a student's motivation to speak is much greater if what he says is "for real" and if he is viewed as an individual whose opinions, feelings, and experiences are considered eminently worthy of attention. These activities focus upon the student as a person with a definite identity, specific interests, feelings, opinions, and experiences that can be shared with others. Because speaking a foreign language in the confines of a classroom often lacks an aura of reality, we want to avoid wherever possible adding further artificiality by asking students to assume roles other than their own.

The *interview cards* and *conversation cards,* used in small groups, make the student the central figure both in terms of behavior (for it is the students rather than the teacher who will be speaking) and content (for students will be talking about themselves). These cards with some minor adaptations can be used at all levels of language study. The questions on the interview cards focus mainly on general personal information while the conversation cards are more closely related to topics, structures, and vocabulary the students are currently studying.

By providing the language necessary to formulate a question (either through direct or indirect phrasing of the question), the necessity for the student to "think up" the question (what to ask and how to phrase it in the foreign language) is eliminated. At the same time, enough flexibility and openness remain enabling students to make statements that are truly personal and authentic. Ideally, our goal is that students will reach the stage where they can formulate their own questions. These conversation and interview cards provide an intermediate step toward that goal.

CONVERSATION CARDS

Conversation cards are used in conjunction with materials presented in the textbook. They exploit either a topic and its related vocabulary (e.g., sports), or a grammatical concept (subjunctive, if clauses, etc.) or a combination of both. For a given topic, whether lexical or grammatical, three cards have been prepared, each containing five to ten questions. For each subject, an attempt is made to have three different sets of questions on the same topic, and to approximate as closely as possible the natural progression of a conversation. No instructions are given about the content of the answer so that students can give either general or personal answers.

The cards are then distributed to students working in groups of three. The teacher explains that the groups function as follows:

1) Student No. 1 asks student No. 2 the first question on his card.
2) Student No. 2 answers the question.
3) Student No. 3 listens and is ready to give assistance whenever necessary or to comment on the answer of student No. 2.
4) Students take turns answering and asking questions.

In contrast to a teacher-directed activity involving the entire class, autonomous groups of three maximize the amount of speaking and listening done by each student and also provide more opportunity for interaction and mutual help. Additionally, student inhibitions are reduced and student initiative in asking and answering questions as well as reacting to the content of both questions and answers is enhanced.

For the beginning student, these questions can be worded in a direct manner.

Example (focusing on use of adjectives):

Quand es-tu content(e)?
Quand es-tu fatigué(e)?
Quand es-tu irrité(e)?
Quand es-tu triste?
Quand es-tu enthousiaste?

At the intermediate level, the questions are indirect, paralleling the well-known directed dialogue technique, with the difference and advantage being that the activity is student rather than teacher centered and directed.

Example (focusing on use of the superlative):

Demandez à x . . .

Quel est le moment de la journée qu'il/elle aime le plus.
Quel est le moment de la journée qu'il/elle aime le moins.
Quelle est l'activité qu'il/elle aime le plus en classe de français.
Quelle est l'activité qu'il/elle aime le moins en classe de français.
Quel a été le jour le plus heureux de sa vie.
Quel a été le jour le plus triste de sa vie.

Example (focusing on use of the imperfect):

Demandez à x ...

si elle/il était généralement heureux(se) quand elle/il était petit(e).
si elle/il avait un jouet préféré quand elle/il était petit(e).
si elle/il préférait être seul(e) ou jouer avec ses amis
qui était son (sa) meilleur(e) ami(e) quand elle/il était petit(e)
quel était pour lui/elle le meilleur moment de la journée

At more advanced levels, conversation cards also invite the participants to elaborate further on their answers by explaining the reasons for opinions, actions, or feelings.

Example (focusing on use of the if clause):

Demandez à x ...

ce qu'elle/il ferait si elle/il était le professeur—pourquoi?
ce qu'elle/il ferait si elle/il était le président—pourquoi?
avec qui elle/il aimerait parler si elle/il avait un secret ou un problème—pourquoi?
si elle/il devait passer une semaine dans un endroit isolé, qui elle/il choisirait pour l'accompagner—pourquoi?
si elle/il pouvait changer sa personalité, quels aspects elle/il aimerait changer—pourquoi?

INTERVIEW CARDS

Interview cards, unlike conversation cards, are not specifically related to any particular unit of a textbook or to the manipulation of a particular structure. Instead they focus on the person interviewed, his personal background, and his interests. All the interview cards, appropriately entitled "Connaissez vos voisins," are specifically designed to enable students to know one another, to relate to one another by using a new system of communication. Exchanges of this sort involve the whole personality of the student. They give a ring of reality to student utterances in the foreign language; they offer the advantage of creating a group atmosphere; and they provide a pool of information that can be drawn upon by teacher and students alike to facilitate further verbal exchange.

Like conversation cards, interview cards can be used at any level. The organizational pattern of the interview cards is hierarchical. They follow a vertical dimension based on the complexity of the language structures that students are able to handle as well as the relative simplicity and

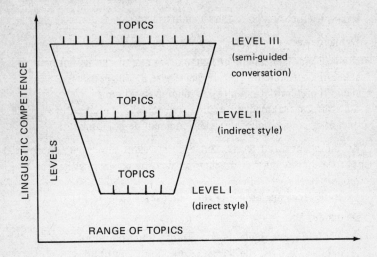

complexity in the wording of the directions. The horizontal progression is based on the premise that the more advanced the student, the greater the variety and complexity of topics available for the interviews.

At the beginning and intermediate levels, students need guidance in phrasing the questions. Thus at an early level, as with the conversation cards, the questions are worded in the direct style, and at the intermediate level they are worded in the indirect style. At more advanced levels, students should possess sufficient linguistic proficiency and autonomy to formulate the questions themselves. Directions at this level simply indicate the nature of the information to be sought.

The very first interviews at each level will focus on name, age, place of origin, and interests.

Level 1:
  Comment t'appelles-tu?
  Quel âge as-tu?
  Où habites-tu?
  Quels cours suis-tu cette année?
  Quelles sont tes distractions favorites?

Level 2:
  Demandez à x . . .

  Comment elle/il s'appelle
  Quel âge elle/il a
  Où elle/il habite

Quels cours elle/il suit cette année
Quelles sont ses distractions favorites
Level 3:
Demandez à x . . .

son nom
son âge
ses cours préférés
le lieu et la date de sa naissance
son adresse
ses distractions favorites

The range of topics for interview cards is almost endless, especially at the more advanced levels. Some subjects that have proven successful are sports, reading habits, future plans, reactions to school and current events, vacation plans, childhood memories, dreams and nightmares, and likes and dislikes.

ROLE OF THE TEACHER

Although the teacher is removed from the actual conversational exchange, his or her presence is invaluable. By moving from group to group, the teacher can inject comments and reactions and can also provide linguistic help in phrasing questions and answers whenever necessary. The teacher must be willing to accept the fact that students may become so involved in the conversation that they will forget his or her presence, which is in itself a sign of success.

APPLICABILITY

Interview cards and conversation cards allow for individualization of instruction within a lockstep classroom. In an individualized classroom the procedure may be somewhat more complex. Here are a few suggestions.

1. Keep a central file of cards arranged according to levels and topics so that students may make their own selections.

2. If possible, have tape recorders available so that students may record their conversations for later review and feedback by the teacher.

3. Solicit suggestions from students for the preparation of new cards.

4. Assign the preparation of cards as individual projects for students who have an interest in a particular area.

SUMMARY

In conclusion, there are several advantages in the use of the conversation and interview cards. These cards . . .

1. Combine in a single activity the skills of listening, reading, and speaking.

2. Allow students to create a mutual help system whereby one student may assist another who is experiencing difficulty in phrasing a question or an answer.

3. Increase students' opportunities to participate actively and to practice in a meaningful and personalized context.

4. Lessen students' inhibitions by allowing them to work in small groups away from the constant control of the teacher.

5. Allow students to communicate with one another, to get to know one another through the foreign language.

6. Place greater emphasis on the ability to communicate (i.e., to request and give information) rather than on grammatical correctness.

7. Give students practice in listening comprehension, i.e., lead students to listen to what others are saying rather than only to what the teacher is saying.

8. Allow students to share experiences and to explore their feelings, reactions, and beliefs towards a variety of situations, thereby adding a value clarification dimension and a truly humanistic quality to the language experience.

FUSION OF THE FOUR SKILLS:
A TECHNIQUE FOR FACILITATING
COMMUNICATIVE EXCHANGE

Robert J. Elkins, Theodore B. Kalivoda *and* Genelle Morain
University of Georgia

From *The Modern Language Journal,* November 1972.

The language teaching profession has become almost obsessed with "The Four Skills." The chant of "listening–speaking–reading–writing" became a sort of incantation to ward off the old grammar-translation bugaboo. We sometimes forget that the ultimate goal in learning a foreign language is not to master the four skills as presented chapter by chapter in the methods book. Rather it is to be able to fuse these skills for genuine communicative exchange.

Unfortunately at the intermediate level, the teacher often continues to concentrate on the individual skills. Such preoccupation with habit formation drills and other manipulative exercises, or with eliciting sterile responses to sterile questions, may account for the distaste for language study expressed by many students. The foreign language class must provide an enjoyable experience that approximates reality. Imaginative fusion of the skills can play a significant role towards this end.

The concept of fusion calls for the interplay of sound and symbol. It is not limited to listening and speaking on one hand and reading and writing on the other, but rather involves a crossing of speech and the written word. It requires listening to what's said, writing what's heard, reading what's written, saying what's read, and varying combinations of each. Fusion facilitates reenforcement of the four skills. It also offers choices in modes of sending and receiving and permits students to interact in a variety of ways.

Several writers have suggested a number of techniques for using partial fusion through different combinations of the four skills:[1] students *listen* to an oral presentation and *write* a resume (two skills); students *listen* and *write,* then *speak* about the main points in the material (three skills). The possibility of fusing all four skills in one exercise, however, has received little attention. This paper presents a technique which has been used at the University of Georgia to provide four-skill fusion in intermediate language classes.

BACKGROUND

Many of us remember the old game of "Gossip" (sometimes called "Rumor" or "Telephone") in which one person starts a message, the next in line passes it on to his neighbor who repeats it to another, and so on around the circle. When the final result is compared to the initial message, there are usually enough discrepancies to evoke a satisfying guffaw. Language teachers have occasionally adopted the technique to provide an interesting form of listening-speaking practice. With the fusion of all four skills as a goal, however, a more dimensional activity is called for. One suggestion for a fusion exercise is outlined below. The reader is assured that its format is not as complicated as first glance might indicate.

"COMMUNICATION": A FUSION TECHNIQUE

Structure

1. The teacher divides the class into groups of six students. Each group represents a miniature communications network.

2. Each group immediately divides into two subgroups composed of three students each. One subgroup is made up of Students One, Two, and Three; the other subgroup includes Students Four, Five, and Six. The task of each subgroup involves communication within its own triad as well as across subgroup boundaries to members of the other triad. (Figure 1)

Figure 1.   A Group

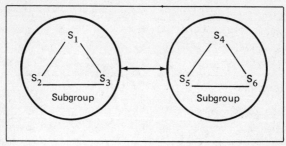

Procedure

1. The teacher gives the lead student in each subgroup (Student One and Student Four) a printed text. Student One receives Story A. Student Four receives Story B. The content of each is totally different, but the length and difficulty are equivalent.

2. The lead students read the stories silently (3 minutes).

3. Student One tells Story A in his own words to the members of his subgroup. Student Four tells Story B to his subgroup (4 minutes).

4. The two students in each subgroup who have listened to the story write it down in summary form. The lead students may answer questions to clarify. The students then exchange their written forms with the two students in the other subgroup (5 minutes).

5. Students Two and Three now read the two versions of Story B which were passed to them. Students Five and Six read the two versions of Story A which they received (4 minutes).

6. Students Two and Three cooperate to tell Story B to Student One. Students Five and Six cooperate to tell Story A to Student Four (4 minutes).

7. The two leaders each paraphrase the story in writing (4 minutes).

8. Student One exchanges his written version of Story B for Student Four's written version of Story A.

9. Students One and Four read aloud the versions they have received and each subgroup decides if the new version approximates the original form (5 minutes).

10. All six members of the group share in discussing the successes and failures of the communications venture (5 minutes).

Diagram

As with most game techniques, the instructions are more complex than the practice. The following diagram may serve to clarify the overall scheme. (Figure 2)

Figure 2.

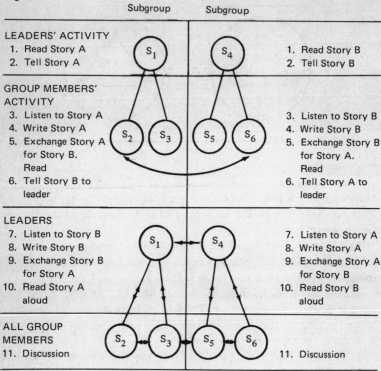

LEADERS' ACTIVITY		LEADERS' ACTIVITY
1. Read Story A	Subgroup S_1 Subgroup S_4	1. Read Story B
2. Tell Story A		2. Tell Story B

GROUP MEMBERS' ACTIVITY

3. Listen to Story A
4. Write Story A
5. Exchange Story A for Story B. Read
6. Tell Story B to leader

S_2 S_3 S_5 S_6

3. Listen to Story B
4. Write Story B
5. Exchange Story B for Story A. Read
6. Tell Story A to leader

LEADERS

7. Listen to Story B
8. Write Story B
9. Exchange Story B for Story A
10. Read Story A aloud

S_1 ↔ S_4

7. Listen to Story A
8. Write Story A
9. Exchange Story A for Story B
10. Read Story B aloud

ALL GROUP MEMBERS

11. Discussion

S_2 ↔ S_3 S_5 ↔ S_6

11. Discussion

STUDENT INVOLVEMENT

A tally of activities involved shows that during the 30-35 minutes devoted to the exercise, each student engages actively in listening, speaking, reading, and writing. He is motivated by the simple desire to communicate accurately—to get it across—to tell it like it is. The end product for each group of six—the final versions of Story A and Story B—may be compared with the end products from all other groups in the class, with the group achieving the most accurate results designated the winner.

The order in which communicative skills are brought into play follows a natural pattern: read, then tell; listen, then write. It is not difficult to imagine situational counterparts in real life: a boy reads an interesting sports item in the newspaper and eagerly recounts it to his friends; a girl listens to a political candidate present his views and jots them down for the school paper.

Some of the fusion activities—listening, reading, writing—call for individual effort. Others demand cooperative communication: synthesizing the two written versions into the best whole and sharing the telling of it; discussing the final version of each story with two others, then analyzing the discrepancies within a group of six. The student not only acts independently, using all four skills, but also jointly in a group-oriented experience.

ROLE OF THE TEACHER

The teacher's first responsibility is to select the material to be used in the exercise. The content of the stories must be perceived by the students as worth communicating. Anecdotes with a surprise twist, short tales of the macabre or bizarre, humorous events from the daily news—all make interesting retelling. Later, students may bring in materials of their own choosing, which makes communication even more relevant. It is suggested that the materials contain for the most part familiar vocabulary and structure. Reading and recounting the contents should be a pleasurable experience. Inclusion of some new words and expressions, however, adds that certain zest which comes only with challenge and experimentation. Students should have more opportunities to explore verbally in a non-threatening situation.

During the fusion exercise the teacher circulates among the groups to help with pronunciation and problems of structure. He keeps an eye on the pacing of subgroups to make sure they are moving through the activity at about the same rate. Once the class gets the feel of the exercise, however, the teacher's role becomes completely unobtrusive. The goal is to establish a communication situation that is self-propelled because it provides its own motivation.

A deterrent to student involvement in communicative exchange may be a feeling of inhibition stemming from linguistic insecurity. Teachers find that four-skill fusion strengthens the self-confidence of the intermediate learner. Students react positively to the chance for communication within moderate guidelines. The fusion technique serves as a bridge between highly structured language practice and liberated expression.

NOTE

1. See the forthcoming publication: Kalivoda, Theodore B. and Robert J. Elkins, "Teaching as Facilitation and Management of Learning," in Dale L. Lange, editor, *Review of Foreign Language Education, Volume 4*. National Textbook Company, Chicago, Illinois, 1972.

THE SELF-DIRECTED DIALOGUE:
A TECHNIQUE
FOR CONVERSATIONAL PRACTICE

Elizabeth Joiner
Winthrop College

From *Foreign Language Annals,* 7:414-416.

In recent years it has become painfully evident to students and teachers alike that the imitation, memorization, and recitation characteristic of audiolingualism have failed to produce fluent speakers of foreign languages. Communicative competence, cited so often as a principal goal of language learning, remains woefully lacking even among many students who have very good pronunciation and who excel in oral pattern practice. It would seem that in order for a student to use the foreign language as a vehicle for communication he would need to have at his disposal not only a certain measure of linguistic ability but also something to say and a reason for saying it. Wilga Rivers has aptly observed, "The foreign-language teacher is faced with a double problem, first, of providing the student with the correct formulae of expression in the new language, and second, of arousing a desire to communicate in that language."[1] This article outlines a technique that this writer has used to stimulate conversation in beginning college French classes.

"Oh, you teach French! Then say something for us in French." This frequent request is puzzling and embarrassing. Although the writer has spoken French for a number of years, she never knows whether to reply by reciting a poem or babbling an inanity. Students must often feel this way when they are divided into small groups and are instructed to converse in the foreign language. Telling them to use sentences similar to those in a recently learned dialogue is undoubtedly helpful, and choosing a "strong" student to lead the discussion may aid in initiating the activity. Nevertheless, free conversations of this sort repeatedly degenerate into an amalgam of embarrassed silence, nervous laughter, and furtive whispering—in English more often than not. This reaction occurs most frequently during the early stages of language learning when students—particularly those who are naturally shy and insecure—appear to want and need some kind of crutch on which to rely.

Such a crutch is supplied through the use of the directed dialogue, an activity generally associated with the audiolingual method.

> The directed dialogue is a controlled conversation between two students stimulated by teacher directions. It consists of a series of commands in which the teacher tells one student to ask a specific question or make a specific statement to another student.[2]

Although this technique provides the student with something to say and a reason for saying it (his teacher told him to), it may be criticized for its artificiality, its rigidity, and the dependence upon the teacher which it fosters.

PROPS FOR SELF-DIRECTED DIALOGUE

Keeping these shortcomings in mind, I have attempted to modify the directed dialogue in such a way as to allow more freedom, to create an atmosphere of *vraisemblance,* and to place the responsibility for communication primarily upon the learner. The resultant technique might be called a self-directed dialogue, an activity that combines a role-playing or simulation strategy with a vehicle for real-communication or contextualized practice. Recent research has provided evidence that such practice can be beneficial in the development of the speaking skill.[3]

The role of the teacher in this activity is principally that of preparing the students linguistically for what they are to say and of providing the props that will serve as crutches, security blankets, or conversation stimuli (if you prefer) for timid talkers. These props should ideally lend credibility to the situation as well. A grocery list, a menu, an identification card, a student's schedule of classes, or an application form for a driver's license or for a job will serve very well as springboards for conversation.

Carte d'Identité

A conversation built around one of these props might proceed in the following manner. After having completed a dialogue concerning the French *carte d'identité,* the teacher uses the overhead projector to show the class what such a form looks like and asks them what questions the prefect of police would have to ask in order to complete the form. (For example, *nom* would require the question, "What is your name?" and *lieu de naissance,* "Where were you born?") Following this discussion, the students are divided into pairs and every student is given an identification card to fill in with information about his partner. In order to fulfill his responsibilities, each student in turn must pose questions and supply answers. As a final activity, various students are asked to tell in narrative form the information obtained in the interview. Again the form serves as a prop by providing an outline for a description which might begin as follows: "Mary Jones is American. She was born in New York. She is twenty years old. . . ."

Restaurant Menu

Having a menu in hand clearly provides a measure of security for the student who is pretending to order·a meal in a restaurant. Indeed, depriving him of this prop in such a situation would be totally unrealistic. The self-directed dialogue built around the menu would be preceded by a discussion, during which the teacher would try to make certain that the students understood the plan of a typical meal, knew the proper wine to order with fish, fowl, or meat, and could pronounce the names of the various foods. Then each student would be given a menu and a blank sheet of paper to be used as an order pad as they take turns being waiter and customer. The final activity might consist of questions by the teacher, such as "What kind of meat dish did Mary order?" or "Did Frank choose red or white wine?" These questions should be answered by the person who took the order.

Large-Group "Mixer"

Imaginative teachers will no doubt be able to add to the props that have already been suggested for dialogues for two speakers. A more lively variation of the self-directed dialogue is based on a "mixer" sometimes used at parties to promote conversation. Each student is given a slip of paper with a list of information that he must find and write down; no two lists are identical. A sample list might read as follows: (1) the name of Jane's brother, (2) the color of Michael's mother's eyes, (3) the number of brothers or sisters Pam has, if any, (4) the age of Christine's father, (5) Paul's preference for movies or television. Should the student find that he has been asked to ask *himself* a question, he is free to ask that question to anyone else he chooses. This activity may be rather noisy because each person talks to a number of others. When the hubbub subsides, the teacher may want to ask random questions based on the lists. For example, the question, "Does Pam have any brothers or sisters?" would be answered by the person who has drawn the list described above.

ADVANTAGES OF SELF-DIRECTED DIALOGUE

As a technique for conversational practice, the self-directed dialogue has a number of advantages. The prop around which the dialogue is built provides sufficient structure for even the beginning student to experience the rewarding feeling that he is able to function satisfactorily in the foreign language in a situation not unlike those encountered in real life. At the same time, the prop does not set upper limits on freedom of expression. These are determined only by the linguistic ability and creativity of the students. (I once overheard a very suave "prefect of police" insert the comment, "You are very pretty, mademoiselle," between "How old are you?" and "Where do you live?") In relation to time, conversations for two provide much more speaking practice for the individual student than he would have in the typical class in which almost all questions and remarks are directed to, or by, the teacher. Psychologically, it is comforting to the student to have something to hold in his hand while he is talking and to be relieved of the pressure of being called on in front of the whole class. Furthermore, the prop used in the self-directed dialogue may be exploited in a number of ways. A prop such as a grocery list, for example, might also furnish the teacher with a point of departure for a culture capsule. In an individualized program, learning packets, each built around a single prop, could be checked out by pairs of students interested in speaking practice.

Despite these strengths, however, it should be pointed out that the self-directed dialogue technique is not appropriate for every situation. It could not, for example, be used during a prereading period because it requires the use of all four skills. It is also important to note that the conversational practice fostered by this technique is primarily question-and-answer practice, whereas much of real life conversation consists of extended series of affirmations. Nevertheless, the self-directed dialogue with its focus on the learner, its flexibility, and its freedom-within-structure format promises to be a valuable technique to be used in conjunction with others in the promotion of communicative competence.

NOTES

1. Wilga M. Rivers, *The Psychologist and the Foreign-Language Teacher* (Chicago: University of Chicago Press, 1964), p. 42.

2. *Teacher's Manual, Audio-Lingual Materials. French: Level One* (New York: Harcourt, Brace and World, 1961), p. 23.

3. See Gilbert A. Jarvis and William N. Hatfield, "The Practice Variable: An Experiment," *Foreign Language Annals,* 4 (May 1970), 401-410.

SKILL-USING ACTIVITIES
IN THE FOREIGN LANGUAGE CLASSROOM

Sidney N.J. Zelson
State University College at Buffalo

From *American Foreign Language Teacher,* Spring 1974. Reprinted with permission of the National Textbook Company, Skokie, Ill.

Students often find a greater source of motivation in activities in which they use their acquired skills in contexts quite beyond the textbook. While they need to participate in skill-gaining activities, they may not get the same satisfaction by finishing one section or another of the text as they will by actually communicating with each other, especially in contexts that are interesting, entertaining, and/or realistic to them.

One such class of language activities would be language games, numerous sources of which are presently available.[1] Another activity of a puzzle-solving nature is a crucigram. It has certain advantages over a crossword puzzle, not the least of which is the ease of its preparation. One may also use the crucigram format asking the student to find a whole sentence. (But in that case it is usually necessary to circle the first letter.) Another common procedure is one in which each student has to add something to the previous utterance: I'm going to take a trip. I will need a_____, a_____, and so on. Next summer I'm going *to work, to swim, to read,* etc. We spend a lot of time *reading, writing, practicing, playing tennis,* etc. If I had the money *I would travel, I would live in Florida, I would buy an island,* etc. So it may be seen that any number of constructions can be used in this way.

Students may be asked to prepare a number of questions to ask their instructor the next day. The questions may deal with items of personal information. After this is done several times the instructor may ask individual members of the class to take his place. The next step may be for the rest of the class to interview two of their classmates. The students who prepare questions may be asked to have a rejoinder prepared for the person who answers. Another procedure is for the instructor to make a statement and for the student to ask a question that would elicit such a response. The student may be asked to use some vocabulary item in a sentence, or finish a sentence that another has started. One may tell the group that he is thinking of something within plain sight and the class is to find out what it is by asking yes-no questions.

Simple role-playing activities are also within reach of the beginning and intermediate class. It may be useful to let the student convey his ideas with gestures as well, perhaps even to insert an English word if he does not know the particular lexical item.[2] The role may come from a reading selection, a dialog, or from some situation the teacher or a student presents. An important element to stress is communication above all else, thus the instructor needs to ignore language errors much more than in the usual activity. The students may also practice the role in English for a few moments, not necessarily so that they may say in the second language what they have just said in English but so that they may help themselves to think in that context.[3]

Role-playing appeals to many groups and offers an infinite range of interesting possibilities. The situations can be realistic, humorous, and imaginative. The same ground rules that were suggested earlier may guide the activity. The following situations are offered in this report.

1) You are Columbus. The crew wants to go back to Spain, and perhaps, to execute you. Talk them out of both. Be eloquent.

2) You would like to borrow money from a bank but the bank officer is reluctant to lend it to you. Try to talk him into making the loan.

3) You are pawning your wrist watch. You would like $50 but the proprietor of the shop just wants to let you have $30. Try to raise him to $50, or as close to $50 as possible.

4) You would like _____ to come to your house for supper on a particular night, but _____ does not seem too interested. You may change days or times but your acquaintance wishes to decline, though it must be done diplomatically. Try to influence the reluctant recipient of your invitation.

5) You have just seen a waiter in your section spill his third plate of food on somebody. At this time he is eager to come and take your order.

You are hoping someone else will come to help you, that he will get off work very soon, or that any other arrangement might be made. Politely decline, stall, or make conversation, though he will insist on bringing you something and on taking your order.

6) You have been waiting in line for some time for a ticket to a play, which will soon begin. A stranger constantly tries to cut in front of you. Each of you is in a great hurry but you must both be polite, in word if not in deed.

7) You work at the customer service counter at a department store. A customer wishes to return something that has obviously been worn and washed a few times. The same person has done this before. Talk to him, and try to refuse him gracefully. Remember, the customer is always right!

8) You are having an interview for a job you have wanted very badly, for the experience, because you want the money, and, thirdly, because a boy or girl in whom you are quite interested also works there. You have just found out that the work will pay one dollar an hour to start, instead of two, as you had expected. Ask for more money from your prospective employer without antagonizing him and closing the door on your employment.

9) A friend of yours has brought her child over, as usual. The child has run amuck in the house and has broken your favorite ash tray. You want to maintain this friendship, but at the same time you are at the limits of your patience. Your friend is often quite defensive about the child, for some reason or another. Talk to her (him), tactfully expressing your concern.

10) Your child is an angel at home (you think) but he gets in trouble in school all the time. You are asked to come to school to talk with his teacher, who isn't impressed with him.

11) Talk your mother or father into letting you borrow the car for the evening. They do not need it but they are "underwhelmed" at the request, even though you have not had an accident or damaged the car. Their reluctance comes from annoyance at some of the minor things that you do, and that you don't do.

12) Ask your brother or sister to let you borrow some article of new clothing. He or she is somewhat reluctant to lend it to you but you really feel that you need it today. He (she) brings up some of your past sins in that area, and you defend yourself, describing the circumstances, and making excuses, etc., and try to persuade him to change his mind.

13) Beg your parent for permission to stay out late on a school night. Even though tonight is a special night, tomorrow is a school day, and 12:30 is just too late.

14) Apologize to a very casual acquaintance for having spilled coffee on his (her) suit. He is really quite unhappy about it and wants money right now to take it to the cleaners, but you don't have the money and want to pay him when he actually has it cleaned. He wants it *now*.

15) You inform the waiter that you were charged for six rolls but you just ate four. The waiter insists that there were six when he brought the plate over to your table. Defend yourself and your wallet.

16) There is a sign on the wall in the restaurant that they guarantee satisfaction. You have just finished your meal and think that their food is terrible. You do not want to pay, having noticed the sign, but you did not complain either, until right now. You try to convince the waiter and the manager that you are really not obligated to pay, and you indicate the sign, but they insist that "the sign has been there before it was their establishment, besides you seemed to like everything."

17) Give excuses to the teacher for not having completed a long-term assignment. Try to get an extension. The teacher is opposed to it, as you have been known to do this before.

18) Prepare a sales pitch for a miraculous fluid you have invented that can do many wonderful things. Be prepared to answer questions about it and to defend yourself against charges of being a fraud.

19) Your brother has brought a girl home to dinner, a girl that he obviously wants to impress. However, he has embarrassed you so many times in a similar situation that you are determined to give him some of the same. Prepare and give your dinner conversation (with all the necessary participants).

20) You have been waiting for an hour and a half for your order. Complain to the waiter. The waiter makes excuses and you challenge them. Be rather obnoxious.

21) (Females) A girl that you and several of your friends despise has married a fellow that you all really like and had thought you would like to get serious about. Gossip about her (any number can play).

22) You are a receptionist for an executive in a large company. Complain about your job to one of your colleagues.

23) You have just entered the principal's office, having been sent there for skipping a class or two. Try to talk your way out of trouble. Be persuasive.

24) Call up another student to inform him that he has an overdue library book (you work there) and he also has a library fine of 43 cents that has not been paid since last Spring. The student tries to put you off. You may coax, cajole, and threaten, but get a promise for the return of the book and the money.

25) You want to watch a particular channel on TV and the rest of the family wants to watch something else. Try to get your way constructively, giving logical reasons, or reasons that seem logical and legitimate. Other members of the family should give counter-arguments.

26) You deliver papers and one of your customers has not paid his bill for several weeks. Try to get him to pay. Your customer tries to put you off in every way possible.

27) This last trick of your sister's (brother's, mother's father's, friend's) is just too much. Complain to another person about it, about the things that person has done in the past, and what you are going to do, or what you really ought to do.

28) You have made the mistake of not establishing a price beforehand with the taxi driver. When you get to your destination he asks you for an exorbitant amount. It is your understanding that there are established prices within one zone of the city and from one zone to another. Try to pay a fair price, about one-fourth of that the driver has asked.

29) Your hotel reservation has been confirmed but upon your arrival you find that there is no room. Argue with the desk clerk and with the manager about giving you a room. You may be obnoxious but not abusive, and they should be sympathetic but firm in their refusal.

The above contexts give opportunity to two or more people to perform in an interactive[4] situation. The students see evidence of their being able to actually communicate in a second language, which is probably one of the strongest kinds of motivation that we have. They may enjoy themselves at the same time.

NOTES

1. William Mackey, Language Teaching Analysis (Bloomington: Indiana University Press, 1967), pp. 441-452. See also MacMillan series; *Invitación al español* and *Invitation au Français,* by DaSilva and Cadoux; Bernard E. Crawshaw, *Let's Play Games in French* (Chicago: National Textbook Company, 1970); Loretta B. Hubp, *Let's Play Games in Spanish* (Chicago: National Textbook Company, 1969); Elisabeth Schmidt, *Let's Play Games in German* (Chicago: National Textbook Company, 1971); Gertrude Nye Derry, *Games for Second Language Learning* (New York: McGraw-Hill, 1966).

2., 3. Sandra Savignon, *Communicative Competence: An Experiment in Foreign Language Teaching* (Philadelphia: Center for Curriculum Development, 1972), pp. 25-32.

4. Wilga M. Rivers, "Talking Off the Tops of their Heads," in *Speaking in Many Tongues: Essays in Foreign-Language Teaching,* expanded 2d edition, Rowley, Mass.: Newbury House, 1976, pp. 21-35. The article suggests a variety of useful areas to pursue.

PERSONALIZING FOREIGN
LANGUAGE INSTRUCTION

David E. Wolfe *and* Leland W. Howe
Temple University.

From *Foreign Language Annals,* vol. 7, no. 1 (October 1973), pp. 81-98.

As a content area in public schools, foreign language is in trouble. Fewer students are studying foreign languages. There may be several reasons for this trouble: (1) fewer students are choosing to go on to college and therefore do not need a language as a prerequisite for a college degree; (2) many colleges are dropping the language requirement from their degree programs; and (3) there is a growing feeling among students that a foreign language and all the work entailed in learning it is irrelevant to their current concerns and problems. Regardless of the reason, if foreign language teachers do not begin to think differently about the role of foreign languages in the curriculum and as a result begin to teach differently, they may soon be without jobs in public schools.

Students, parents, and educators are calling for more humane schools; many of them want to put an end to the factory system kind of schooling that treats children and young adults as products to be molded into shape and packaged for the world of business and industry. The cry is for schools which provide personalized teaching and learning and in which the primary responsibility of the teachers is to attend to the concerns and needs of the students, to help them become better decision makers and better functioning human beings. Teachers increasingly are beginning to read and listen to such people as Abraham Maslow, Carl Rogers, and Arthur Combs, who for some years have been writing about a new educational psychology that goes beyond the mechanistic approaches of behaviorism and has, as its central focus, the human being—his "self," his perceptions, his beliefs, and his values. The goals of this new "humanistic" education, according to Maslow, are (1) to help the student achieve his full potential, (2) to help the student discover his own identity, (3) to help the student become a self-directed learner who makes wise choices about his own learning, and (4) to help the student meet his basic psychological needs for security, belonging, dignity, love, respect, and self-esteem.[1]

How can the teaching and the learning of a foreign language contribute to these humanistic goals? Certainly they can not if teachers continue to try to cover the book—to be on chapter 22 during the second week of February. The "coverage syndrome" is characteristic of "factory education." With the pressures of getting the students through the material, the teacher has little time for the concerns or interests of the students because these often seem to divert attention from the skills to be acquired or the content to be covered. Students in such classes, therefore, feel as though they are being processed, and it is this feeling that the students of the 1970's overwhelmingly reject.

ROLE OF FOREIGN LANGUAGES

Foreign languages have a distinct role to play in the humane curriculum. In addition to satisfying a utilitarian need if students wish to travel or live in a foreign country, the study of a foreign language can be a sensitizing experience for students. Herein lies a central function of languages in the school curriculum. A foreign language can be used as a means for students to "get outside" themselves and, from a new perspective, examine their lives, their values, and their ways of thinking. This new perspective is that of a different culture and its way of conceptualizing, thinking about, and verbalizing things through its own language. Thus, language can serve the same purpose as do the humanities—philosophy, art, literature, and music. It can provide students with mirrors in which they can study themselves—who they are, where they are going, where they want to go, and how they can get there.

Languages, if they are to provide sensitizing experiences for students, will have to be approached in a manner considerably different from the simple coverage of the book, drill and recitation, programmed instruction, or the other approaches that constitute the bulk of instructional pedagogy in the conventional contemporary school. Indeed, foreign language teachers will need to learn new teaching strategies and techniques that involve using the language to help students talk about and, from the perspective of this language, examine their own beliefs, attitudes, values, interests, and concerns.

The purpose of this article is to delineate some strategies and techniques for using language as a sensitizing experience to the students' own values, beliefs, and life-styles. The writers have translated the strategies into two languages—French and Spanish—using a step-by-step format in which the purposes, procedures, and follow-up activities are outlined in sufficient detail for the classroom teacher to use them as they are or adapt them for his own use. The aim is to help students find answers to the questions, Who am I? and What do I want to be?

These strategies can become games or gimmicks if they do not have any framework that has a goal. Used out of context, they can become nonpurposeful "time killers." Their power will be diminished if the teacher does not know the values or goals of humanistic education. Therefore, caveat emptor.

VALUES GRID

The Values Grid is an activity that helps the student discover the steps he must take in order to develop stronger and clearer values.[2]

Procedure

1. Distribute a copy of the Values Grid to the students.

2. Choose some pertinent current issues with the students; for example, la guerre en Indochine, la ecología, la légalisation des avortements, las elecciones presidenciales, la discipline dans cette école.

3. Ask the students to write next to these issues two or three key words that summarize their ideas on the issue. The seven numbers heading the columns on the right-hand side of the paper represent the following questions:

1. ¿Está *orgulloso*(a) de su punto de vista?
   Est-ce que vous êtes *fier* de votre point de vue?
2. ¿*Affirmó publicamente* su punto de vista?
   Avez-vous *affirmé publiquement* votre point de vue?
3. ¿Ha formado su opinión sobre otras *alternativas*?
   Avez-vous choisi votre avis parmi d'autres *alternatives*?

4. ¿Ha formado su opinión depués de *mucha consideración* sobre
   los pros y contras?
   Avez-vous fait votre choix après avoir *considéré* le pour et le
   contre?
5. ¿Ha formado su opinión *libremente*?
   Avez-vous choisi votre avis en toute *liberté*?
6. ¿Ha *manifestado* sus creencias?
   Avez-vous *agi*, ou *fait* quelque chose selon vos croyances?
7. ¿Ha manifestado su opinión *varias veces*?
   Avez-vous agi *plusieurs fois* selon vos croyances?

These seven questions can be written on the chalkboard or projected by
the overhead projector. The students write the key words (those that are
italicized) at the top of each column. These seven questions are then
answered in relation to the issue. If there is a positive response, a check is
marked in the appropriate box. If there is no positive response, the box is
left blank.

Table 1   Values Grid

Issue	*1*	*2*	*3*	*4*	*5*	*6*	*7*
1. Les avortements							
2. La ecología							
3. La discipline							
4. Las elecciones							
5. La guerre							
Etc.							

Follow-up
After checking the boxes the students may form small groups to discuss
one of the issues, their position on it, and how it did or did not meet the
seven valuing processes. (The more check marks there are for each issue
the stronger the value tends to be for the individual.) The students must
know that they are being asked not to defend their beliefs, but to
evaluate the means by which they arrived at their convictions and the
strength of their beliefs. The students can also discuss orally before the
class or write a short paper about the experience and what they learned
about themselves. They should be encouraged to keep logs and compare
their first entries with those of a future date.

TWENTY THINGS I LIKE TO DO
VEINTE COSAS QUE ME GUSTAN HACER
LES VINGT CHOSES QUE J'AIME BIEN FAIRE

This strategy allows the students to ask themselves if they are really getting out of life what they want (Simon, p. 30). Are the lives they are leading based on what they want or do they wait for fate to decide for them? In order to help students discover who they are and to help them build the kinds of lives they want to live, teachers must help them discover their values and desires. This strategy serves that purpose.

Procedure

1. Distribute sheets of paper to the students and have them number from 1 to 20 down the middle of the paper.

2. Instruct them, "Háganme el favor de escribir las veinte cosas que más les gustan hacer en su vida." "S'il vous plaît, écrivez les vingt choses que vous aimez mieux faire dans votre vie."

To encourage the students to get started, the teacher might say, "Estas cosas pueden ser sencillas o importantes. Si prefieren, piensen en las estaciones del año y en las cosas que les gustan hacer." "Ces choses peuvent être simples ou importantes. Si vous voulez, pensez aux saisons de l'année et aux choses que vous aimez faire pendant ces saisons." The first time this strategy is attempted, the students may have difficulty in knowing where to begin. It is appropriate for the teacher to offer one or two suggestions from his own life by saying, "Me gusta dar un paseo después de cenar." "J'aime bien aller aux matchs avec mon ami(e)."

The teacher also, perhaps publicly on the chalkboard, draws up a list of twenty things he likes to do. Some students will have difficulty in finding twenty things they like to do; others may be able to list many more. It is important to tell the students, "Si vous avez moins de vingt ou plus de vingt, ça ne fait rien." "No importa si ha escrito más de o menos de veinte." This activity alone may take ten to fifteen minutes to complete, depending on grade and language level.

3. When the students have finished, tell them to write the following symbols, letters, or numbers in the left column of their papers. (Depending on the language competence of the students, the teacher will have to choose carefully or edit the following suggestions.)

a. ¡Ponga un $ si la cosa cuesta más de $3-5 hacerla!
   Mettez un $ si la chose vous coûte plus de $3-5 à faire!
b. ¡Ponga una S si prefiere hacer la cosa solo(a)!
   Mettez un S si vous préférez faire la chose tout(e) seul(e)!

c. ¡Ponga una P si prefiere hacer la cosa con otras personas!
   Mettez un P si vous préférez faire la chose avec d'autres personnes!

d. Las letras PL están colocadas al lado de las que tiene que planear.
   Les lettres Pl sont mises à côté de celles qui doivent avoir un plan.

e. ¡Ponga N-5 al lado de las que no habria hecho hace cinco años! (N = no)
   Mettez NP-5 à côté de celles que vous n'auriez pas faites il y a cinq ans. (NP = ne . . . pas)

f. Al lado de las cinco más importantes, escriba del 1-5. Uno para la más importante o más preferida.
   Ecrivez les numéros 1-5 à côté de celles qui sont les plus importantes. Le numéro un sert pour la plus importante ou la plus aimée.

g. ¡Indique el día o la fecha la última vez que hizo la cosa indicada!
   Indiquez la dernière fois que vous l'avez faite en écrivant le jour ou la date.

It is clear that some of these steps can be used at all levels; others can be used only after certain grammatical points have been learned. A guideline for teachers to remember is that they never should go beyond the point at which the students would be frustrated by the instructions. The procedure can be altered to The Fifteen Things I Like to Do or The Ten Things I Like to Do. Experience has shown that some students may not have more than ten things they like to do. This activity may continue for two to three days depending upon the age group and the amount of time each day the teacher wishes to spend on it. Therefore, the students should keep Values Notebooks to which they can refer for future classroom use and which allow them to see how their interests may change or broaden during the year.

Follow-up

1. Have the students write short compositions (100-150 words) or make oral presentations based on one of the activities they like to do best. The following questions may serve as guidelines for students: With whom? When (what time)? Where? Under what conditions?

2. Have two or three students write their lists on the board, eliminating those items that are too personal. (The teacher may also write his list on the board.) This second step can be followed by the Public Interview (see below).

Other Procedures

¡Ponga una I si la cosa le es íntima!

Mettez un I si cette chose est intime!

¡Ponga una T para las cosas que los otros pensarán son típicas!

Mettez un T pour les choses que les autres penseront sont typiques!

¡Ponga una M para las cosas que quiere mejorar!

Mettez un M pour les choses que vous voulez (faire) mieux ou améliorer!

¡Ponga una F para las cosas que no estarán en su lista cinco años de ahora!

Mettez un F pour les choses qui ne seront pas sur votre liste cinq ans dès aujourd'hui!

VALUES VOTING

This strategy is a simple but quick means to let students publicly affirm their convictions (Simon, p. 38).

Procedure

1. Read aloud a series of questions always preceded by ¿Cuántos de vds. . . . ? or Combien parmi vous . . . ?

Examples:

¿Cuántos de vds. van a la iglesia? ¿A cuántos les gusta ir?

¿Cuántos de vds. ven la televisión más de tres horas al día?

¿Cuántos de vds. peinsan que a los "teen-agers" les sea permitidos comprar su propia ropa?

Combien parmi vous vont voter pour le même parti politique que leurs parents?

Combien parmi vous croient qu'il faut tricher de temps en temps?

At first, students may all vote alike or the way they think the teacher wants them to vote. As they learn that no punitive action is connected with their choices, they tend to be more discriminating in their voting. The teacher should also vote, but should wait a second or two after the class has committed itself in order to avoid influencing the students' choices. Students raise one hand for being in favor, two hands for being strongly in favor. They indicate negative votes by putting thumbs down—one hand for being against, two hands for being strongly against.

They fold their arms to show they are undecided; their taking no action means they pass.

2. Encourage the students to submit their own questions. The teacher should use these questions on subsequent days. Motivate the students to ask their questions in the foreign language (orally) or write them on three-by five-inch cards. Values Voting can be used as a feedback device for the teacher. For instance, ¿A cuántos les gusta la novela que estamos leyendo? Combien parmi vous aiment écrire une petite composition le lundi? This brief information can help a teacher alter activities that students find unproductive or uninteresting.

Students vary in their preferences for learning activities. Some will not understand the question and will not vote on it. It is suggested that the question first be read in the target language and then be translated for those who did not understand. The voting questions may also be written on clear plastic sheets and shown with an overhead projector. The questions are covered with a sheet of paper, revealed one at a time, and read aloud. This method allows eye- and ear-oriented students to understand the question. The questions can also be reproduced on a ditto machine so that every student has a copy. As many as twenty or thirty voting questions can be duplicated in this manner. On any specific day the teacher may randomly select five or ten questions or select a student to direct the activity.

This technique can be used at the beginning of the class in lieu of the "warm-up." It tends to lose its value after five or ten minutes. Depending on the desires of the students, Values Voting can be followed by discussion of one or two of the questions so that students can tell why they voted for or against an issue.

RANK ORDER

Rank Order gives the students practice in choosing among alternatives and in publicly affirming, explaining, or defending their choices (Simon, p. 58).

Procedure
1. Prepare several questions based on the vocabulary and structures that the students know. The questions are worded so that students have to make a value judgment.

2. Give two, three, or four choices for each question. At first, younger students or beginning pupils may have to be given only two

choices. It may be the first time they have ever been given alternatives, or the linguistic comprehension load may be too much the first or second time and, therefore, they may not be able to retain all of the options given. As students develop more maturity in selecting or listening ability, the number of alternatives is increased.

3. Read the question and choices and ask several students to give their rankings. A student should always be given the opportunity to pass by saying, "No quiero responder" or "Je ne veux pas répondre." After six or eight students have responded, the teacher gives his ranking. As with Values Voting, discussion may follow so that students may give their reasons for their responses. At this time participation is open to all, regardless of prior participation. The teacher may also duplicate the questions and the alternatives and distribute them. All students should write their rankings, and six or eight should share theirs with the class.

Sample Rank Order Questions:

¿Dónde quisiera pasar el sábado?

(1) en la playa (2) en el parque (3) en un almacén

Comment apprenez-vous le mieux?

(1) en écoutant le professeur (2) en petits groupes (3) an étudiant seul(e)

Imaginez que vous êtes un Noir! Dans quels pays voudriez-vous vivre?

(1) aux Etats-Unis (2) au Sénégal (3) en France

¿Qué prefiere hacer después de cenar?

(1) preparar mis tareas (2) ver la televisión (3) llamar por teléfono a un(a) amigo(a).

The teacher may ask students to prepare other Rank Order Questions and Alternatives in order to bring a different focus to the process. This strategy also can be used to motivate students for a lesson—on a dialogue, a reading passage, a literary work, or a news event. For example, a recent news item may tell of a dictator as having taken over a country. Using the guidelines outlined above, the teacher may ask, "Si tuviera que vivir en un país de habla española que tiene un dictador, en cuál viviría vd.?

(1) en España (2) en Cuba (3) en la Argentina

Students may not have enough information to vote thoughtfully, and they may follow up this question with a research project on one or all three countries by reading articles in English or Spanish or by interviewing native speakers of these countries if they are available in the community. After completing the project, they report to the class and another vote is taken. Using the target language, students should give reasons for changing or not changing their votes.

UNFINISHED SENTENCES

This strategy helps the students discover and explore some of their attitudes, beliefs, actions, convictions, interests, aspirations, likes, dislikes, goals—in short, their values indicators (Simon, p. 241). Students often emerge from this activity with growing awareness of their developing values.

Procedure
1. Provide the students with a list of unfinished sentences. These can be presented on the overhead projector or duplicated so that students can keep them in their logs.
2. Have the students keep written records of their stand with the date indicated. The records serve as reminders of the ways their beliefs and goals may change.

Large or small group oral work is an excellent follow-up activity. For teachers interested in ideas for ways to have more personal oral work of a small group nature in individualization of language learning, most of the strategies in this paper are appropriate.

Examples:
1. Los sábados me gusta . . .
   Le samedi j'aime . . .
2. Si tuviera veinticuatro horas que vivir yo . . .
   Si j'avais vingt-quatre heures à vivre . . .
3. Me siento bien cuando . . .
   Je suis à mon aise quand . . .
4. No quiero que mis niños . . .
   Je ne veux pas que mes enfants . . .
5. Lo que busco en la vida es . . .
   Ce que je cherche dans la vie c'est . . .
6. Antes yo era . . .
   Autrefois j'étais . . .
7. Nunca he querido . . .
   Je n'ai jamais aimé . . .

The teacher may also use unfinished sentences as feedback by saying, "La cosa que me gustó más de esta unidad es. . . ." Or after reading about

French influence in West Africa, the teacher may say, "Je ne savais pas que. . . ."

This technique is similar to one offered by George Brown entitled "Sentences Completion Form: Who Am I?" Brown suggests that the students, after completing the sentences, list five single words that they can associate with themselves now.[3]

PUBLIC INTERVIEW

A Public Interview allows a student to have the undivided attention of the class for ten minutes and to affirm and explain publicly his stand on various values issues (Simon, p. 139). A positive side result of the interview is that students rethink about or discuss what they have said outside of class. Experience shows that this strategy is particularly favored by students.

Procedure
1. Ask for volunteers to be interviewed about their beliefs, values feelings, and actions.

2. Have a volunteer sit at the front of the class while the teacher interviews him from the back of the class.

3. Explain the following ground rules and make certain students adhere to them. The teacher may ask the student-volunteer any question about any aspect of his life or values. The student must answer honestly. The student has the option of passing on any question he does not wish to answer by saying "no quiero responder." The student ends the interview at any time by saying, "L'entretien est fini," or "La entrevista está terminada." The student then may ask the same questions of the teacher. The same ground rules apply except that the teacher may not pass on a question unless the student did.

4. Ask questions that are based on known vocabulary and structures. Sometimes it will be necessary to teach an additional vocabulary item or two. However, students should be encouraged to stay within their linguistic limits.

Sample Interview Questions:
1. ¿Va vd. a la iglesia? ¿Le gusta ir? ¿Qué aprende vd.?
2. Si vd. fuma, ¡díganos por qué!
3. Si pudiera tener cualquier edad, ¿Cuál le gustaría tener?
4. ¿Vd. se pelea con sus hermanos? ¿Por que se pelean? ¿Por qué se pelean sus padres y vd.?

5. ¿Por qué cree vd. en Dios?
6. ¿Qué marca de pasta dental usa vd.? ¿Cómo llegó a usarla?
7. ¿Cuál es su curso preferido en la escuela, y por qué?

I URGE TELEGRAMS/LETTERS TO THE EDITOR

These two similar strategies give students the opportunity to make a statement about something that is personal to them (Simon, p. 262, p. 264). Moreover, public affirmation is one of the processes in developing values.

Procedure

1. For the I Urge Telegrams strategy, give the students four- by six-inch cards or, for greater realism, blank Western Union telegraph forms.

2. Have the students choose a real person (in the country where the language under study is spoken) and write a telegram to that person beginning with "Insisto en que vd. . . ." or "Je tiens à ce que . . ." in fewer than twenty-five words. Students should be encouraged to send the telegram to that person.

3. For the Letters to the Editor strategy, have the students write letters to the editor of a newspaper or magazine in the country where the language is spoken.

4. Have carbon copies made, read to the class, and posted for all to see. A request is made of the editor to send copies of any printed letters that actually appear. These letters are then clipped to the carbon copies of the original letters.

A recent event that might have impelled students of French to write a letter to the editor happened in Quebec Province, Canada. The Minister of the Interior allegedly was going to allow open season on the wolf population because the wolves were a menace to farmers who had domestic animals. Students also might be interested in writing a letter to a French newspaper protesting or defending nuclear weapons testing. In addition to affirming a belief publicly, students also learn cultural differences of letter writing. The students read their telegrams or letters to the class, giving their reasons for their feelings and explaining how they arrived at that position.

THE FALL-OUT SHELTER PROBLEM

This is a simulated problem-solving exercise that is more suited for fourth or fifth level classes or intermediate college conversation courses (Simon,

p. 281). It raises a host of values which the student must attempt to work through in a rational manner. It poignantly illustrates how our values differ, and how we often have trouble listening to people whose beliefs are different from our own.

Procedure
1. Divide the class into groups of five to seven students.

2. Describe the situation to the students. Your group comprises members of a department in (Bonn, Mexico City, Paris) which has responsibilities for disaster planning. Suddenly World War III breaks out and atomic bombs are dropping everywhere. An emergency call from a bomb shelter center informs you that there are ten persons requiring shelter and there is a supply of food and water sufficient for only six people for the three-months waiting period required for elimination of the radiation hazard. Within the next half hour you must decide which six persons are to go into the shelter. No decision at the end of this time period means that all then will die. The following facts are the only information available about the ten persons:

Señora de 23 años, encinta.
Policía con pistola.
Indio revolucionario en su segundo año de estudios médicos.
Cura de 54 años.
Chica de la universidad.
Bio-químico.
Escritor de 42 años.
Campesino de 31 años.
Atleta olimpiaco: excelente en todos deportes.
Actriz, cantante, bailarina.
P . . . du "Moulin Rouge," enceinte.
Gendarme avec pistolet.
Etudiant africain, assez révolté, deuxième année à la Faculté de Médecine.
Auteur/historien fameux, 42 ans.
Savant en bio-chimie.
Petit fonctionnaire, 30 ans.
Curé d'un petit village, 50 ans.
Jeune fille lycéenne.
Danseuse, cantatrice.
Athlète arabe, très fort en tous sports.

3. Have students discuss in the target language the pros and cons about keeping the six people.

4. Give time warnings of fifteen, ten, five, and one minutes.

5. Ask the groups to give their lists of the six who stay and give their reasons for their choices.

The teacher may then ask, "How well did you listen to the others?" "Did you let others influence your decision?" "Were you so stubborn that the group could not reach a decision?" "What does your selection say to you about your values?" A short position paper can be written for follow-up.

THE PERSONAL LIFE MAP

This technique may be used to show how students can understand and express their feelings (Brown, p. 36).

Procedure

1. Instruct the students to close their eyes and draw imaginary maps on their eyelids.

2. Explain that for each student the left side of the map is where he is now in his life—his feelings, and his awareness of himself. The right side of the map is where he wants to go in his life. In the middle there are obstacles that block him from where he wants to go. The student is to determine whether anything can be done about these obstacles now. If not, he is not to change them but to be aware of them and how he feels about them.

3. Have students use the target language to share their experiences orally with the class or have them write brief papers (100-200 words). Such papers should not be graded, only corrected. The content should not be corrected to avoid destroying the value-clarifying effect of such an assignment.

THE HERE AND NOW WHEEL

The Here and Now Wheel allows the students to express their inner feelings in one word. Often these inner feelings help to explain overt behavior.

Procedure

1. Have the students draw circles and divide them into four or five pie-like sections.

2. Have the students write in each of these sections one word that identifies their feelings. In a beginning class this activity can be

completed in English to identify some of the words the students will need to know in the foreign language. These words are left on the board for a few days until the students no longer have need of them.

3. Ask volunteers to take one of their "feelings" words and formulate a sentence. For example, "Ahora estoy *enojado* porque acabo de sacar una mala nota en un examen de inglés." Or, "Je suis *ennuyé* parce que je n'aime pas cette classe." For variety, this technique can be used at the beginning of the class for one week, in the middle for the next week, and at the end for the third week. It can also be completed at the beginning and end of the same class session. Students can see how their feelings can change over a period of time or within the short span of one class session. The wheel can be dittoed with the day of the week written above each wheel. Students can see how feelings can vary from day to day. It is important to remember not to penalize students for giving their true feelings. The information obtained can help the teacher to understand why students behave as they do and to gain information about things the teacher is doing in class and how they affect the students. Some sample words students may need to know are cansado(a), enojado(a), triste, contento(a), aburrido(a), feliz, orgulloso(a), hambriento(a), heureux(se), fatigué(e), ennuyé(e), malade, fâché(e).

SOME FINAL THOUGHTS

These strategies are only a few of the many that can be developed and used to make the teaching and learning of foreign languages more humane and personally involving for the student. It is important to stress again, however, that these are not games to be played in the classroom by the uninitiated teacher. One does not develop a humane and personally involving classroom overnight by simply playing a few values games. The trust level in the classroom must be sufficiently high before students will risk sharing the kind of personal information called for in many of the strategies. Trust builds in a classroom when students are encouraged to risk only a very small amount at first and when they find that what they have to say is well received and accepted by both the teacher and other students. The teacher may find students reluctant, or even resistant, to participating in the strategies in the beginning. However, when students find it is safe to share their feelings and thoughts, involvement is likely to soar.

It is important to keep several guidelines in mind. (1) Participation should always be voluntary. (2) Students must listen to each other and respect the rights of others to differ in their views. (3) The content of the strategies should not be used for grading purposes. If the teacher follows these three guidelines and seriously cares about and respects the opinions of the students, the strategies should work well in the classroom.

The writers recommend that the uninitiated teacher seek training in humanistic education approaches before doing much of this kind of teaching. Additional information about the training of foreign language teachers in humanistic approaches to education is available from the authors or from The Philadelphia Center for Humanistic Education, 355 Wadsworth Avenue, Philadelphia, Pa. 19119.

NOTES

1. Abraham H. Maslow, *The Farther Reaches of Human Nature* (New York: The Viking Press, 1971), chapter 13.

2. Sidney B. Simon, Leland W. Howe, and Howard Kirschenbaum, *Values Clarification: A Handbook of Practical Strategies for Teachers and Students* (New York: Hart Publishing Company, 1972), p. 35.

3. George I. Brown, *Human Teaching for Human Learning: An Introduction to Confluent Education* (New York: The Viking Press, 1971), p. 61.

TOPICS FOR DISCUSSION AND/OR ACTION RESEARCH

GAMES AND PUZZLES

1. The guessing games described by Joiner are activities which involve the entire class at once while those described by Omaggio and Gibson rely on a small-group framework. Which do you think would be more successful with your students? Try out one whole-class game and one small-group game and analyze your students' reactions to each.

2. Gaming techniques are often used by counselors and language arts teachers to develop awareness of group dynamics. Ask a counselor or language arts teacher in your school to share with you sources of such techniques and to help you to select one to develop for your class.

3. The guessing game strategy is, to a certain extent, language-centered in that each game is designed to elicit a particular type of word (numbers, colors, dates) or structure (He is singing). In contrast, some of the other activities are idea-centered. What structures and vocabulary do you think would occur in (a) a jigsaw puzzle game built around pictures of objects, (b) a strip story based on narrative material, (c) a group culture capsule?

4. If you are hesitant about trying small-group games and puzzles with an entire class, ask a few students to meet with you during a free period for a run-through in which you can identify potential problems. Or start with a more advanced smaller class and work backward to the larger beginning classes. Try to identify the level which is most responsive to this type of activity.

5. Work through a jigsaw picture puzzle of your own. Think of words the first letter of which when combined would spell *chien* (French) or *katze* (German) or *libro* (Spanish) or *table* (English). Draw or find pictures to illustrate.

6. Think of some applications of the guessing games to your particular situation. (a) Select items from your textbook vocabulary which could be used for price-guessing. (b) Create a guessing game to practice names of professions and trades. (c) Compile a list of verbs from your textbook which could be used in a charade-type guessing game.

7. What problems would arise if you used a story which combined narration and dialogue in a strip story activity? What type of narrative would be most suitable for a strip story?

SMALL-GROUP TECHNIQUES

1. Using Paulston's classification of drills (mechanical, meaningful, communicative), classify the 8 procedures presented in the Disick article.

2. The activity listed by Disick as *Procedure 2* is similar to that described by Bonin and Birckbichler. The teacher might also write the questions on a transparency (instead of dittoed sheets or cards) and ask students to arrange their desks so that only the interviewer can see the questions. Would the activity be essentially the same in all three formats? Try them and compare the results.

3. Procedure 1 and Procedure 8 as presented by Disick involve topics for written work and speaking practice. Would the same topics be suitable for both activities? Could your students speak and/or write successfully on these topics: "What is happiness?" "Which is more important, a car or a telephone?" "Is a college education worth the money it costs?" Use your textbook to make a list of topics for written and oral communication. How does talking about a topic ("Tell me about yourself") differ from talking within a question-response format ("Answer these 10 questions about yourself")?

4. The conversation cards described by Bonin and Birckbichler are built around student interests and may vary in difficulty according to language level. Write a conversation card for beginning students about *sports* then adapt it for intermediate and advanced students.

5. Write a set of conversation or interview cards for use with a certain chapter of your textbook or to review several chapters. Does your textbook have personalized questions which may serve as a starting point? Start a file of cards for use year after year.

6. Elkins, Kalivoda, and Morain say that their technique was designed for use with intermediate students. Could it be used with beginners or advanced students? What changes would have to be made?

7. Collect a file of short narrative material for use in the fusion technique. Check for timing and level of difficulty by asking a couple of students from your class to read them silently.

8. The fusion technique is set up for groups of six. If your class did not divide evenly into such groups, what could you do? Would the effect be the same?

9. Think through the fusion technique carefully. What do the other students do during the time that the lead students are reading the stories? What implications does this have for the type of reading to select, the choice of lead students, etc.? Do "dead spaces" occur during the working out of this technique?

10. Discuss the role of the teacher in the small-group activities described in these three articles. What must the teacher do in the way of outside preparation? In the classroom what must the teacher do before, during, and after each activity?

STRATEGIES FROM THE HUMANISTIC EDUCATION MOVEMENT

1. Which type of activity, the self-directed dialogue or role-playing, could be used more successfully with elementary language students? Why?

2. Try to classify the role-playing activities suggested by Zelson into levels of difficulty—beginners, advanced beginners, intermediates, advanced intermediates, etc. To verify your classification, try the activities with students of different ability levels.

3. Zelson's suggestions for role-playing relate primarily to one person's role in a conversation. Write role-play cards to be given to the other persons involved in the conversation. For the first simulation, you would want to write two or three cards for the various crew-members.

4. Role-play cards may be designed to practice a particular grammatical structure. An example would be: "You've just met a person who thinks everything s/he owns is the greatest and the best. The only way you can handle this person is to top everything s/he says." This, of course, would practice the superlative. Try to write role-play cards for practice of the negative.

5. Like the other types of activities described in Part II, simulations and role-playing call for realistic use of language; however, these activities force the student to assume a different personality. What types of

students might have difficulty in participating in a role-playing activity? How might you prepare the class for role-playing?

6. Consider the advantages and disadvantages of the following approaches to role-playing: (a) Two or three students come to the front of the class, draw role-play cards, look over them for a moment, then create the situation described on the cards while the other students in the class observe; (b) Role-playing is done in groups of two or three. All members of the class are talking at once while the teacher circulates among them; (c) The above techniques are combined. All students go through the small-group practice; then certain students are called on to act out the scene in front of the class with new partners.

7. In Part I, Palmer describes a communicative practice drill which involves the creation of situations for which the students must provide appropriate remarks. Would it be possible to use such a drill to prepare the student for less-structured role-play? Try to create a communicative practice drill for the superlative. Then try to create a situation for role-play which would encourage use of the superlative.

8. Create 5-10 conditional sentences for your students to complete. Use *Example 2* from the Wolfe and Howe article as a model.

9. Values clarification activities involve a risk factor which is not present in some of the other activities presented in this section. Arrange the activities described in the article in rank order according to the amount of personal risk involved.

10. Analyze each activity from the point of view of skills (listening, speaking, reading, writing) involved. "Values Voting," for example, will basically involve listening comprehension but may be modified to involve reading and writing as well.

11. Analyze each activity from the point of view of grammatical categories involved. "Twenty Things That I Like to Do" would, of course, focus on verbs.

12. Write 7-8 questions which might be used for a "Public Interview." How does this technique differ from the interview card technique described by Bonin and Birckbichler?

13. Some of the values clarification techniques require considerable ability to express oneself. Should students be allowed to switch to their native language if they cannot find the words in the target language? Which is more important in this kind of activity, the meaning expressed or the words used to express it?